The
JUMBO
BIBLE
WORDSEARCH
COLLECTION

BARBOUR
PUBLISHING, INC.
Uhrichsville, Ohio

Published by Barbour Publishing, Inc.
         P.O. Box 719
         Uhrichsville, Ohio 44683
         http://www.barbourbooks.com

 Member of the
Evangelical Christian
Publishers Association

Printed in the United States of America.

The JUMBO BIBLE WORDSEARCH COLLECTION

Word Search 1

ADAM AND EVE AND THE
GARDEN OF EDEN

Why did Adam and Eve try to hide from God? Find out in Genesis 2-3.

BEGUILED

BOTH NAKED

BREATH OF LIFE

CHERUBIM

CURSED

DEEP SLEEP

EAST

ENMITY

EUPHRATES

FIG LEAVES

FLAMING SWORD

FOUR RIVERS

FRUIT

GAVE NAMES

GIHON

GOOD AND EVIL

HELP MEET

HIDDEKEL

HID FROM GOD

MADE APRONS

MAN OF DUST

MOTHER OF ALL LIVING

NOT ASHAMED

PISHON

RIB

SERPENT

TREE OF LIFE

TREE OF THE KNOWLEDGE

WOMAN

```
M A E B T C B R E A T H O F L I F E
A O D N L E K E D D I H I E U F G U
D G T O M H V S I D J G K W D D A P
E L X H M I T N F O L P Y E E R V H
A Q Z S E N T R R E S A M L T O E R
P U B I E R O Y A V C A W G F W N A
R W D P X M O V Y D H O Z O A S A T
O D R M G B E F E S N C U O D G M E
N E E O A S F K A K G R H D C N E S
S L D I E N A T E L R J T A H I S K
L I N M F N O H N I L E O N E M P G
Q U A C H N T F V R E L S D R A T H
U G M T U F V E D M W I I E U L S X
Y E O Z O R R A P U B J C V B F D T
E B W E F S S L G K S H L I I O M J
D E E P S L E E P K N T L L M N M O
F R U I T H N P D O Q P N O H I G Q
T R E E O F L I F E R B T A S R I B
```

Word Search 2

ALL ABOUT CHURCH

AISLE

ANNOUNCEMENTS

ASSEMBLY

ATTENDANCE

AUDITORIUM

BAPTISM

BIBLE

BRETHREN

CHOIR

CHORUS

CHRISTIAN

COLLECTION PLATE

COMMUNION

CONFESSION

CONGREGATION

DEACON

ELDER

FELLOWSHIP

GOD

"HALLELUJAH!"

HOLY SPIRIT

HYMNAL

INVITATION

JESUS

MEMBER

MINISTER

PEOPLE

PEWS

PRAISE

PRAYER

PREACHER

RELIGION

REPENT

REVIVAL

SALVATION

SCRIPTURES

SERMON

SERVICE

SONGBOOK

SONG LEADER

SUNDAY SCHOOL

TEACHER

VISITORS

WORSHIP

```
A N N O U N C E M E N T S R O T I S I V
S I L J M S I T P A B M P E W S C N K I
S O S O N G L E A D E R P L G Q H D R N
E S L L T M I M A J N U E V O W O X P V
M Y O R E L I G I O N Z Q T A G I B R I
B C O P R E A C H E R R P I H S R O W T
L D H R E F T G S H E E I N J R K T P A
Y L C E P M U A N D O P O Q M R E S R T
T V S B E U W V L P W I X U Y L Z N A I
A H Y M N A L E L P T B I C B D X E I O
F A A E T G K E E A N R H I J Y K R S N
N L D M C L I C V K O O B G N O S E E O
O L N M Z N I L N T P A I Q B L R V R I
I E U P S V A T I U C R E T S I N I M S
N L S V R S W D E A C O N X C Y D V O S
U U Z E U A U A N B E C S U S E J A N E
M J S R D A Y E F E P I H S W O L L E F
M A O F H G S E R U T P I R C S H L I N
O H O L Y S P I R I T T E A C H E R O O
C H R I S T I A N O I T A G E R G N O C
```

Word Search 3

ALL ABOUT GOD

Below are 39 words found in the book of Psalms that describe God. Find them in the puzzle.

ABUNDANT MERCY
 (Psalm 51:1)

BLESSES (Psalm 147:13)

COMPASSIONATE
 (Psalm 78:38)

DELIVERER (Psalm 18:2)

ENDURES FOREVER
 (Psalm 135:13)

FEARED (Psalm 96:4)

FORGIVING (Psalm 86:5)

FORTRESS (Psalm 18:2)

GLORIOUS (Psalm 76:4)

GOODNESS (Psalm 31:19)

GRACIOUS (Psalm 86:15)

HIDING PLACE (Psalm 32:7)

HIGHLY EXALTED
 (Psalm 47:9)

HOLY (Psalm 22:3)

HOPE (Psalm 39:7)

JUDGE (Psalm 7:8)

JUSTICE (Psalm 89:14)

KIND (Psalm 145:17)

KNOWLEDGE (Psalm 139:6)

MAJESTIC (Psalm 8:1)

MIGHTY (Psalm 24:8)

OUR MAKER (Psalm 95:6)

POWERFUL (Psalm 29:4)

PRECIOUS (Psalm 36:7)

REDEEMER (Psalm 19:14)

REFUGE (Psalm 7:1)

RIGHTEOUS (Psalm 11:7)

ROCK (Psalm 18:2)

SANCTUARY (Psalm 73:17)

SLOW TO ANGER
 (Psalm 86:15)

STEDFAST LOVE (Psalm 6:4)

STRENGTH (Psalm 18:1)

SUN (Psalm 84:11)

THE MOST HIGH (Psalm 7:17)

TRUSTWORTHY (Psalm 111:7)

UNDERSTANDING
 (Psalm 147:5)

UPRIGHT (Psalm 33:4)

WONDERFUL (Psalm 139:14)

WONDROUS DEEDS
 (Psalm 40:5)

```
S T R E N G T H G I H T S O M E H T
Y D E L I V E R E R E K A M R U O A
R W E G R A C I O U S S E N D O O G
A O G L O R I O U S B V C S L E P D
U N D E R S T A N D I N G L U C R E
T D E L R E D E E M E R Y O F A E B
C R L F U N V R G R G C J W R L C S
N O W B U F A E I D R H U T E P I T
A U O S L E R G R E U P S O W G O E
S S N D F E H E M O R J T A O N U D
S D K Y N T S T D I F I I N P I S F
E E J L E I N S G N K S C G L D M A
R E N O P A K H E H O P E E Q I O S
T D U H D R T R U S T W O R T H Y T
R S G N I V I G R O F R E F U G E L
O T U H I G H L Y E X A L T E D S O
F B C I T S E J A M I G H T Y U N V
A K C O R C O M P A S S I O N A T E
```

Word Search 4

ANANIAS AND SAPPHIRA

What happened when Peter questioned Ananias and Sapphira about the proceeds of the sale of their property? Find out in Acts 5:1-11.

ANANIAS

APOSTLES' FEET

BROUGHT ONLY PART

BURIED

CARRIED OUT

DIED

FELL DOWN

GREAT FEAR

HEART

HOLY SPIRIT

HUSBAND

KEPT PROCEEDS

LIE

PETER

PIECE OF PROPERTY

SAPPHIRA

SATAN

SOLD

THREE HOURS

WHOLE CHURCH

WIFE

WRAPPED

YOUNG MEN

? According to Solomon's proverb, what is in Wisdom's right and left hands?

Long life is in the right and riches and honor are in the left. Proverbs 3:16

```
Y T R E P O R P F O E C E I P
W R H M R T S O L D P G N S V
H A N A T A S I U I R D D A S
O P P Y O U N G M E N E J P Q
L Y V O E K O A A D E I E P A
E L B I S G L T N C X R C H T
C N L Y D T F H O I F U H I U
H O O I L E L R U Z A B E R O
U T W R A P P E D S J S F A D
R H M R Q T K E S U B P I N E
C G R V P X R H T F G A W S I
H U F E L L D O W N E W N Z R
Y O K J T A P U E L B E H D R
I R F C Q E M R H E A R T N A
O B T I R I P S Y L O H D K C
```

Word Search 5

BAPTISM OF JESUS

Find out what happened when John the Baptist baptized Jesus in Matthew 3:13-17.

BAPTIZED

BELOVED SON

CAME FROM GALILEE

HEAVENS OPENED

HOLY SPIRIT

JESUS

JOHN THE BAPTIST

JORDAN

LIKE A DOVE

SAW SPIRIT OF GOD

VOICE FROM HEAVEN

WENT UP FROM WATER

What did John the Baptist eat?

Locusts and wild honey. Matthew 3:4

W	S	A	W	S	P	I	R	I	T	O	F	G	O	D
E	L	G	D	E	Z	I	T	P	A	B	M	H	I	N
N	E	V	A	E	H	M	O	R	F	E	C	I	O	V
T	O	L	P	I	H	T	I	J	Q	L	R	K	S	T
U	T	L	I	U	M	J	U	N	V	O	W	O	X	I
P	Y	P	Z	K	A	Q	K	B	J	V	C	J	D	R
F	H	E	A	V	E	N	S	O	P	E	N	E	D	I
R	E	R	L	S	F	A	R	G	T	D	H	S	I	P
O	J	U	M	V	K	D	D	L	W	S	M	U	N	S
M	O	X	N	P	A	Q	Y	O	R	O	T	S	U	Y
W	S	Z	V	N	W	A	O	X	V	N	Y	B	Z	L
A	B	C	P	V	Z	W	Q	D	A	E	C	E	D	O
T	S	I	T	P	A	B	E	H	T	N	H	O	J	H
E	E	L	I	L	A	G	M	O	R	F	E	M	A	C
R	E	F	R	X	A	L	C	K	M	B	Y	S	G	F

Word Search 6

BEATITUDES

Locate and loop only the words underlined in these verses found in Matthew 5:3-11 (RSV).

"Blessed are the poor in spirit, for theirs is the kingdom of heaven.
Blessed are those who mourn, for they shall be comforted.
Blessed are the meek, for they shall inherit the earth.
Blessed are those who hunger and thirst for righteousness, for they shall be satisfied.
Blessed are the merciful, for they shall obtain mercy.
Blessed are the pure in heart, for they shall see God.
Blessed are the peacemakers, for they shall be called sons of God.
Blessed are those who are persecuted for righteousness' sake, for theirs is the kingdom of heaven.
Blessed are you when men revile you and persecute you and utter all kinds of evil against you falsely on my account.
Rejoice and be glad, for your reward is great in heaven, for so men persecuted the prophets who were before you."

```
R K I N G D O M E R C I F U L
T I R I P S L N R U O M A M R
N S G R E A T O T B M P L Q D
S T E H P O R P T A F E S S R
D A L G T B L A T H O S E A A
B E F O R E I P O O R E L K W
C O G L X N O E D E T R Y E E
S R I E H T V U K A E U K L R
D E I F S I T A S G D P I B K
E S M C L R M H C N O V N R T
S N E V A E H T H C E D D E S
S O N D C H E R E R O S S T R
E S F A G N H A A I L U S T I
L R E J O I C E R R E G N U H
B P E R S E C U T E D J M T T
```

Word Search 7

BIBLICAL ANIMALS

ANTELOPE	HART
APE	HEDGEHOG
ASP	HORSE
ASS	HYENA
BADGER	LEOPARD
BEAR	LION
CAMEL	LIZARD
CAT	MOLE
CATTLE	MOUSE
CHAMELEON	PYGARG
CHAMOIS	ROEBUCK
CONEY	SCORPION
DOG	SERPENT
DROMEDARY	SHEEP
FERRET	SWINE
FOX	WEASEL
FROG	WHALE
GECKO	WILD BOAR
GOAT	WILD OX
HARE	WOLF

```
D R A P O E L H E D G E H O G
Q R A E B R P S A Y E N O C S
L I O N T G R A G Y P U R V T
C H A M E L E O N M O U S E E
F A N W E X H Y E Z A I E B R
L C T D J D E K L B A D G E R
O F E G L H A I O L U J M L E
W I L D B O A R M K I C L A F
C F O M K N T O Y P A Z K H O
H R P C Q N G O A T R N A W X
A O E S E C T P T U T E V R O
M G W P S S A L E X R N Y P D
O Z R B O A E M C E A I D O L
I E R A H E A N E Y H W G F I
S C O R P I O N G L E S A E W
```

17

Word Search 8

BIBLICAL BODIES OF WATER

ARABAH	MEDITERRANEAN
DEAD SEA	NILE
ENROGEL	PISHON
EUPHRATES	PLAIN
GIHON	RED SEA
HULEH	SALT
JORDAN	SEA OF GALILEE
KISHON	TIGRIS

What are the four rivers in the Garden of Eden?

Pishon, Gihon, Tigris, and Euphrates.
Genesis 2:11-14

```
A R A B A H L J O R D A N
M A N K U O M E H L P A I
Q N E L R A E S D A E D L
S O E S T P F Q U N V E E
W H X R D Y S Z A O A U B
L C N D T E F R E H G P H
E I U O J V R K W I L H M
G N X P H E O S Q G S R K
O R Y U T S I V T W T A I
R X Z I Y R I Z A L B T S
N C D E G F A P G B A E H
E E L I L A G F O A E S O
M H T J C G D I P L A I N
```

Word Search 9

BIBLICAL CITIES

ACCAD	ENDOR	NOPH
ADORAIM	EPHESUS	PETRA
ANATHOTH	GAZA	ROME
ANTIOCH	GOMORRAH	SAMARIA
ANTIPATRIS	HAM	SARDIS
APOLLONIA	HAMATH	SELA
AROER	HARAN	SELEUCIA
ASHDOD	HEBRON	SHILOH
BABEL	JERICHO	SIDON
BETHEL	JERUSALEM	SMYRNA
BETHLEHEM	KERIOTH	SODOM
CAESAREA	LAODICEA	SUCCOTH
CORINTH	NAIN	THESSALONICA
DAMASCUS	NAZARETH	THYATIRA
DIBON	NEBO	TYRE
DOTHAN	NINEVEH	UR OF THE
EMMAUS	NIPPUR	CHALDEES
		ZOAN

```
H N A B E T H L E H E M H E B R O N
T A N A T H O T H N E M S M Y R N A
H I T J O H K P D L N I A N L Q M Z
Y D I B O N E O A D B A L E S H O A
A N O D I S R S A L A R T E P A M R
T E C T N P U C S G B O E M N R O E
I B H J H R C I Q A E D R M E R Y T
R O A A E A D B N Z L A C A D O E H
A F M J G R N T H A I O J U K M L C
I M A A A N I O H A R A N S P O R A
C Q T S R P S C H E V E N I N G E E
U T H H A O E U H T N I R O C C V S
E A F T T H E A P O L L O N I A B A
L C R H T O I R E K D G E D E M O R
E I T F U A C V N O P H O L I H S E
S M O D O S U C S A M A D O D H S A
W R U P P I N X U Y L E H T E B A Z
U B D E P H E S U S A M A R I A C M
```

Word Search 10

BIBLICAL FRUITS, VEGETABLES ,
AND GRAINS

BARLEY	LEEKS
BEANS	LENTILS
CORN	MELON
CUCUMBERS	POMEGRANATE
FIG	RYE
GRAPES	WHEAT

 Paul planted the seed, Apollos watered it,
but who made it grow?

God. 1 Corinthians 3:6

```
E  L  E  E  K  S  L  C  A  M  F
Y  T  B  N  D  O  C  O  S  I  E
R  Q  A  S  E  P  A  R  G  F  R
G  J  S  N  H  T  E  N  I  U  L
S  K  Y  W  A  B  A  R  L  E  Y
N  O  L  E  M  R  L  X  N  M  N
A  Z  O  U  A  P  G  T  B  Q  C
E  R  C  D  T  S  I  E  F  E  U
B  U  G  V  J  L  H  W  M  I  X
C  K  Y  M  S  L  Z  A  N  O  B
W  H  E  A  T  C  O  D  P  E  P
```

Word Search 11

BIBLICAL GEMS AND STONES

AGATE	JACINTH
ALABASTER	LAPIS
AMETHYST	LAZULI
BDELLIUM	LIGURE
BERYL	ONYX
CARBUNCLE	PEARL
CHALCEDONY	RUBY
CHRYSOLITE	SAPPHIRE
CORAL	TOPAZ
EMERALD	

 Of the three kings who reigned during the rebuilding of the temple in Jerusalem, who was in power when it was finished—Cyrus, Darius, or Artaxerxes?

Darius. Ezra 6:15

```
A  G  A  T  E  L  O  S  M  Y  N  B
E  L  C  N  U  B  R  A  C  N  P  D
M  Z  A  P  O  T  U  P  Q  O  O  E
E  T  R  B  S  U  B  P  T  D  N  L
R  S  L  V  A  W  Y  H  X  E  Y  L
A  Y  Z  A  L  S  H  I  Y  C  X  I
L  H  A  Y  P  T  T  R  B  L  C  U
D  T  R  D  N  I  E  E  G  A  F  M
H  E  T  I  L  O  S  Y  R  H  C  I
B  M  C  J  L  L  A  R  O  C  K  M
L  A  Z  U  L  I  N  P  A  Q  B  R
J  O  P  E  A  R  L  I  G  U  R  E
```

Word Search 12

BIBLICAL HERBS AND SPICES

ALOE	GARLIC
ANISE	HYSSOP
BALM	LOVE APPLE
CASSIA	MINT
CORIANDER	MUSTARD
CUMMIN	MYRRH
DILL	SAFFRON
FRANKINCENSE	SPIKENARD
GALL	

If a cheerful heart is good medicine, what does a crushed spirit do?

Dries the bones. Proverbs 17:22

```
H  A  D  R  A  T  S  U  M  B  H  E
R  C  I  M  J  D  P  K  N  E  S  L
R  E  S  I  N  A  I  F  L  N  G  P
Y  O  D  P  T  Q  K  R  E  S  L  P
M  U  W  N  V  C  E  C  N  L  L  A
C  E  O  L  A  X  N  Y  I  Z  A  E
I  A  D  S  B  I  A  D  M  C  G  V
L  E  S  F  K  G  R  H  M  I  L  O
R  I  B  N  J  M  D  O  U  I  K  L
A  S  A  F  F  R  O  N  C  N  N  O
G  R  L  P  U  X  Z  A  Y  V  Q  T
F  R  M  S  W  T  H  Y  S  S  O  P
```

Word Search 13

BIBLICAL INSECTS

ANT	GRASSHOPPER
BEE	HORNET
BEETLE	HORSELEECH
CATERPILLAR	LICE
CRICKET	LOCUST
FLEA	MOTH
FLY	PALMERWORM
GNAT	WORM

 This servant of Saul's told David that Saul was survived by a son named Mephibosheth. Who was he?

Ziba. 2 Samuel 9:3

```
R  A  L  L  I  P  R  E  T  A  C
H  E  B  E  E  L  M  S  F  N  R
O  C  P  O  Q  I  U  P  L  R  I
R  S  E  P  T  C  U  W  E  Y  C
N  V  X  E  O  E  M  L  A  L  K
E  U  A  L  L  H  T  O  Z  F  E
T  W  O  R  M  E  S  B  T  C  T
D  G  A  H  E  I  S  S  E  H  F
J  N  K  B  L  O  M  R  A  N  P
T  P  A  L  M  E  R  W  O  R  M
T  A  N  G  Q  S  U  T  R  H  G
```

Word Search 14

BIBLICAL MEN AND WOMEN
WHOSE NAMES BEGIN WITH
THE LETTER "A"

AARON	AMOS
ABEDNEGO	AMRAM
ABEL	ANANIAS
ABIATHAR	ANDREW
ABRAHAM	ANNA
ABSALOM	ANNAS
ADAM	APOLLOS
ADONIJAH	AQUILA
AGABUS	ARCHELAUS
AHAB	ARCHIPPUS
AHASUERUS	ARISTARCHUS
AHAZ	ARTAXERXES
AHAZIAH	ARTEMAS
AHIJAH	ASA
AHIMELECH	ATHALIAH
AMAZIAH	AUGUSTUS CAESAR
AMON	

```
A G A B U S U A L E H C R A A
A B I A T H A R M A R M A R H
R A S H A J I N O D A L A C A
O H M A T H A L I A H S N H Z
N I O S L O A N D R E W P I I
S J G U A O B A H A D A Q P A
E A E E N O M A C A S C L P H
X H N R D O I S L A M E O U C
R N D U S Z U I M O F L P S E
E A E S A T U E G A L E H Q L
X S B M S Q T R I O H B S J E
A A A U A R T K S U A A V L M
T M G N A N W Z A H A O R P I
R U X A N A N I A S Y A Z B H
A R I S T A R C H U S A N N A
```

Word Search 15

BIBLICAL MEN AND WOMEN
WHOSE NAMES BEGIN WITH
THE LETTER "B"

BAASHA

BALAAM

BARABBAS

BARAK

BARNABAS

BARTHOLOMEW

BARTIMAEUS

BATHSHEBA

BELSHAZZAR

BENJAMIN

BOAZ

Of course, Jacob had 12 sons, but who was his only daughter?

Dinah. Genesis 34:1

```
B   A   R   T   I   M   A   E   U   S   A

E   A   H   S   A   A   B   L   B   M   C

L   N   R   D   O   E   O   P   F   A   Q

S   S   G   T   R   H   A   S   B   I   T

H   A   J   U   H   K   Z   E   A   V   L

A   B   W   M   X   O   H   N   L   Y   K

Z   A   O   Z   P   S   L   B   A   Q   A

Z   N   C   R   H   D   S   O   A   E   R

A   R   U   T   F   T   G   V   M   I   A

R   A   A   N   I   M   A   J   N   E   B

W   B   A   R   A   B   B   A   S   B   W
```

Word Search 16

BIBLICAL MEN AND WOMEN
WHOSE NAMES BEGIN WITH
THE LETTER "C"

CAESAR

CAIAPHAS

CAIN

CALEB

CARPUS

CLEOPAS

CORNELIUS

CRISPUS

CYRUS

Saul had a son named Jonathan, of course. But
can you name his four other children?

1 Samuel 14:49

Ishvi, Malki-Shua, Merab, and Michal.

34

L	C	A	I	A	P	H	A	S
C	C	A	E	S	A	R	U	A
A	M	A	H	P	N	I	O	P
R	I	Q	L	J	L	K	R	O
P	L	S	N	E	M	T	O	E
U	P	U	N	Q	B	V	N	L
S	U	R	Y	C	R	W	I	C
X	O	S	Y	T	Z	U	A	B
C	R	I	S	P	U	S	C	V

Word Search 17

BIBLICAL MEN AND WOMEN
WHOSE NAMES BEGIN WITH
THE LETTER "D"

DAN

DANIEL

DAVID

DEBORAH

DELILAH

DEMETRIUS

DORCAS

DRUSILLA

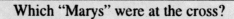

Which "Marys" were at the cross?

*Mary, Jesus' mother; Mary Magdalene; Mary, James'
mother; and Mary, Cleopas' wife.
Mark 15:40; John 19:25*

```
B   D   L   C   D   A   V   I   D
M   E   E   D   O   E   N   E   R
P   L   F   B   Q   G   M   R   U
D   I   S   H   O   E   T   I   S
O   L   J   U   T   R   K   V   I
R   A   L   R   W   M   A   X   L
C   H   I   D   A   N   Y   H   L
A   U   Z   N   A   P   B   O   A
S   Q   L   E   I   N   A   D   C
```

Word Search 18

BIBLICAL MEN AND WOMEN
WHOSE NAMES BEGIN WITH
THE LETTER "E"

EBED-MELECH	EPHRAIM
ELAH	ERAPHRODITUS
ELAM	ERASTUS
ELEAZER	ESAU
ELI	ESTHER
ELIJAH	EUNICE
ELIMELECH	EUODIAS
ELISABETH	EUTYCHUS
ELISHA	EVE
ENOCH	EZEKIEL
ENOS	EZRA
EPAPHRAS	

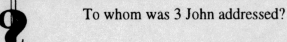

To whom was 3 John addressed?

Gaius, John's friend.
3 John 1

```
E  L  A  M  E  U  T  Y  C  H  U  S
L  B  S  O  N  E  R  A  S  T  U  S
A  C  E  Z  E  K  I  E  L  T  D  A
H  F  E  D  G  A  H  S  I  L  E  R
T  E  S  A  M  C  B  D  H  E  I  H
E  L  T  A  O  E  O  C  U  L  M  P
B  E  H  N  I  R  L  N  J  I  D  A
A  A  E  K  H  D  I  E  A  J  L  P
S  Z  R  P  M  C  O  R  C  A  E  E
I  E  A  N  E  F  H  U  G  H  S  Z
L  R  E  V  E  P  I  L  E  O  A  R
E  L  I  M  E  L  E  C  H  P  U  A
```

Word Search 19

BIBLICAL MEN AND WOMEN
WHOSE NAMES BEGIN WITH
THE LETTER "G"

GAD

GAIUS

GALLIO

GAMALIEL

GERSHOM

GIDEON

GOLIATH

Who is the father of lies?

The devil. John 8:44

```
L   T   G   I   D   E   O   N

U   E   V   A   W   I   X   N

Y   B   I   Z   L   G   C   O

G   G   O   L   I   A   T   H

A   D   A   P   A   D   Q   S

I   G   E   S   R   M   F   R

U   T   G   V   H   U   A   E

S   M   O   H   S   R   E   G
```

Word Search 20

BIBLICAL MEN AND WOMEN
WHOSE NAMES BEGIN WITH
THE LETTER "H"

HABAKKUK	HAZAEL
HAGAR	HEROD
HAGGAI	HEZEKIAH
HAM	HIRAM
HAMAN	HOSEA
HANNAH	HULDAH

What is the last word in the Bible?

Amen. Revelation 22:21

```
H  A  H  A  D  L  U  H  L
A  E  A  E  S  O  H  K  B
M  C  Z  M  D  N  U  O  H
H  E  A  E  P  K  N  F  A
A  Q  E  G  K  R  A  H  G
N  S  L  A  T  I  M  I  A
N  J  B  H  I  R  A  M  R
A  A  D  O  R  E  H  H  U
H  A  G  G  A  I  K  V  L
```

Word Search 21

BIBLICAL MEN AND WOMEN
WHOSE NAMES BEGIN WITH
THE LETTER "J"

JACOB	JEZEBEL
JAIRUS	JOAB
JAMES	JOANNA
JAPHETH	JOASH
JASON	JOB
JEHOAHAZ	JOCHEBED
JEHOIADA	JOEL
JEHOIAKIM	JOHN THE APOSTLE
JEHOIACHIN	JOHN THE BAPTIST
JEHORAM	JONAH
JEHOSHAPHAT	JONATHAN
JEHU	JOSEPH
JEPHTHAH	JOSHUA
JEREMIAH	JOSIAH
JEROBOAM	JOTHAM
JESSE	JUDAH
JETHRO	JUDAS

```
J E H O S H A P H A T B O C A J
E O A J A J E H U L B J E S S E
H R H M O C A H D N L E O T J H
O H T N E S S P A N F O S G A O
I T H M T O I H H P H I Q I I I
A E P A J H T A R E T J M L R A
C J E H T A E K H P T E A E U D
H U J T N M V A A W R H R O S A
I J N O J O A B P E Y P O J A Z
N O J J C R E O J O N A H Q D A
O B O S P H A D U J S T E J U H
S U A Q T V E R W A C T J A J A
A B S N S L E B E Z E J L M D O
J E H P E S O J E F U H V E G H
J O A N N A I W L D J X M S K E
J E H O I A K I M A O B O R E J
```

Word Search 22

BIBLICAL MEN AND WOMEN
WHOSE NAMES BEGIN WITH
THE LETTER "M"

MACHIR	MELCHIZEDEK
MAGOG	MENAHEM
MAHLON	MEPHIBOSHETH
MALACHI	MESHACH
MALCHUS	METHUSELAH
MANASSEH	MICAH
MARK	MICHAL
MARSENA	MIDIAN
MARTHA	MIRIAM
MARY	MOAB
MARY MAGDALENE	MORDECAI
MATTHEW	MOSES
MATTHIAS	

```
M E P H I B O S H E T H Q U M
E R W E H T T A M S V X T A E
L M A L C H U S W M B Z R E T
C E Y B A Z A L D M C Y I M H
H S E M L M I R I A M R H A U
I H O A A I P C H A A A C H S
Z A I R M C A J G S R M A L E
E C C S L H U D M V T N M O L
D H O E X A A P Y R H Q Z N A
E A S N D L B M A N A S S E H
K T D A E R U E O M O A B D G
V G Z N W H O A X S I J Y E O
K M E N A H E M B L E C M P G
D N K R A M F Q E R O S G P A
M I D I A N H S A I H T T A M
```

Word Search 23

BIBLICAL MEN AND WOMEN
WHOSE NAMES BEGIN WITH
THE LETTER "N"

NAAMAN	NATHAN
NABOTH	NATHANAEL
NADAB	NEBUCHADNEZZAR
NAHASH	NECHO
NAHOR	NEHEMIAH
NAHUM	NICANOR
NAOMI	NICODEMUS
NAPHTALI	NOAH

The Book of Philemon is a post card from Paul
to Philemon. On whose behalf was it written?

Onesimus, Philemon's runaway servant.
Philemon 10

```
N A P H T A L I A N A H O R
B E H K N P C N I L O D A O
N A H A S H E A J M F Z G N
Q Y F E R Z G D S A Z T B A
U C H J M V D A W E I E X C
S K R W Z I L B N M S N T I
U N U X A O A D P V Y A Q N
M N A O M I A H B H K H C A
E D I L Q H E J O F N U G H
D M R T C N T H O A P M S T
O U A U V B C O M W N C X A
C Y B D G E Z A B E H O F N
I E I R N J A O S A K P A L
N A T H A N A E L M N Q N H
```

Word Search 24

BIBLICAL MEN AND WOMEN
WHOSE NAMES BEGIN WITH
THE LETTER "S"

SALOME	SHALLUM
SAMSON	SHALMANESER
SAMUEL	SHEM
SARAH	SILAS
SAUL	SIMON
SENNACHERIB	SOLOMON
SHADRACH	STEPHEN

 Of the 12 spies who were sent to explore Canaan, which two gave invasion a thumbs up?

Joshua and Caleb. Numbers 14:6-9

R	S	A	L	O	M	E	L	W	J	B
E	A	S	M	X	H	N	O	M	I	S
S	M	S	O	N	S	S	Y	R	S	I
E	S	H	O	L	A	A	E	Z	A	K
N	O	E	P	L	O	H	M	A	U	M
A	N	M	I	Q	C	M	B	U	L	U
M	R	S	C	A	L	P	O	R	E	L
L	S	O	N	S	D	M	S	N	Q	L
A	T	N	E	H	P	E	T	S	E	A
H	E	F	N	T	U	S	A	R	A	H
S	H	A	D	R	A	C	H	V	G	S

Word Search 25

BIBLICAL MEN AND WOMEN
WHOSE NAMES BEGIN WITH
THE LETTER "T"

TAMAR	TIMAEUS
TEBAH	TIMOTHY
TERAH	TIRHAKAH
THADDAEUS	TITUS
THOMAS	TROPHIMUS
TIGLATH	TUBAL

How many sons did Gideon have?

71. Judges 8:30, 31

52

```
T  I  R  H  A  K  A  H  L  T
I  S  T  I  M  A  E  U  S  A
G  M  U  U  B  H  N  U  P  M
L  V  B  E  N  C  M  I  O  A
A  D  A  W  A  I  O  J  T  R
T  E  L  P  H  D  X  K  E  S
H  Y  M  P  L  Q  D  F  R  U
T  H  O  M  A  S  R  A  A  T
S  R  Z  G  T  E  B  A  H  I
T  I  M  O  T  H  Y  T  A  T
```

Word Search 26

BIBLICAL MEN AND WOMEN
WHOSE NAMES BEGIN WITH
THE LETTER "Z"

ZAAVAN	ZEBADIAH
ZABAD	ZEBEDEE
ZABBAI	ZEBINA
ZABBUD	ZEBUDAH
ZABDI	ZEBUL
ZABDIEL	ZEBULUN
ZACCHAEUS	ZECHARIAH
ZACCHUR	ZEDEKIAH
ZACHARIAS	ZEPHANIAH
ZACHER	ZERAH
ZADOK	ZERUBBABEL
ZAHAM	ZIMRI
ZALMON	ZIPPORAH
ZALMUNNA	ZOPHAR
ZATTU	ZORAH
ZAZA	ZUR

```
Z E C H A R I A H R E H C A Z
E E I D B A Z N U L U B E Z E
D A R L Z N Y R E G S L P S B
E I U U A B O I A A Z A Z A U
K R H B B C D P I H A R O Z D
I M C E B B D R Q Z P K H Z A
A I C Z A E A Z I P P O R A H
H Z A Z I H F B R E A D Z A A
A G Z S C B I R E M N A Q V I
I H Z A H A M D H L O Z T A N
D A Z I U C E Z A L M U N N A
A R D U B B A Z J V L R D J H
B E K W E Z E B I N A E N N P
E Z F Z A B A D L X Z K O Z E
Z A C C H A E U S M U T T A Z
```

Word Search 27

BIBLICAL MOUNTAINS

ATLAS	NEBO
EBAL	OLIVE
EPHRAIM	PISGAH
GERIZIM	SEIR
GILBOA	SINAI
GILEAD	TABOR
HERMON	TAURUS
HOR	ZAGROS
HOREB	ZION

Who said, "I see people; they look like trees walking around?"

A blind man who Jesus healed. Mark 8:24

G	I	L	B	O	A	I	B	J	H
I	E	P	H	R	A	I	M	O	P
L	B	R	C	N	L	P	R	O	I
E	A	L	I	Z	Q	D	S	L	S
A	L	S	E	Z	A	V	A	I	G
D	T	R	I	M	I	G	F	V	A
S	U	O	G	N	O	M	R	E	H
E	N	B	E	R	O	H	I	O	N
I	H	B	O	T	A	U	R	U	S
R	O	B	A	T	S	A	L	T	A

Word Search 28

BIBLICAL MUSICAL INSTRUMENTS

CITHERN

CORNET

CYMBALS

HARP

LUTE

LYRE

PIPE ORGAN

PSALTERY

TIMBREL

TRUMPET

 Who said, "What is man that you are mindful of him?"

David. Psalm 8:4

H	D	C	I	T	H	E	R	N
Y	A	O	L	M	E	T	A	S
R	F	R	N	Y	U	G	L	A
E	O	N	P	G	R	A	E	V
T	H	E	W	O	B	E	R	P
L	U	T	E	M	I	Q	B	X
A	J	P	Y	R	Y	B	M	D
S	I	C	S	K	C	E	I	Z
P	T	E	P	M	U	R	T	L

Word Search 29

BIBLICAL PLANTS AND SHRUBS

BOX

BROOM

BULRUSH

CAMPHIRE

GOURD

HEMLOCK

HENNA

MYRTLE

PAPYRUS

RUSH

THISTLE

 The tree of the knowledge of good and evil was the downfall of Adam and Eve, as we well know. What was the name of the other symbolic tree in Eden?

The tree of life. Genesis 2:9

H	E	M	L	O	C	K	D	A
S	E	Y	E	R	M	T	N	T
U	F	R	N	U	X	N	S	H
R	O	T	I	S	E	G	U	I
L	H	L	P	H	U	Y	R	S
U	Q	E	V	I	P	Z	Y	T
B	J	B	R	O	O	M	P	L
D	R	U	O	G	K	R	A	E
L	S	W	A	X	C	B	P	C

Word Search 30

BIBLICAL TREES

ACACIA	OAK
ALMOND	OIL
BALSAM	OLEASTER
BOX	PALM
CEDAR	PINE
CHESTNUT	PLANE
CYPRESS	SHITTAH
EBONY	SYCAMINE
ELM	SYCAMORE
FIG	TEIL
FIR	TEREBINTH
HOLM	WILD OLIVE
JUNIPER	WILLOW
MULBERRY	

```
W  I  L  L  O  W  K  A  O  C  B  O
A  I  C  A  C  A  L  G  Y  H  L  I
B  A  L  S  A  M  I  P  X  E  I  L
N  E  V  D  O  F  R  O  A  S  E  Z
S  O  B  N  O  E  B  S  M  T  T  W
Y  J  D  O  S  L  T  P  U  N  P  H
C  U  Q  S  N  E  I  X  L  U  I  A
A  N  M  Y  R  Y  R  V  B  T  N  T
M  I  L  H  T  N  I  B  E  R  E  T
I  P  A  O  C  E  D  A  R  L  S  I
N  E  P  L  A  N  E  T  R  I  M  H
E  R  O  M  A  C  Y  S  Y  U  F  S
```

Word Search 31

BIBLICAL WEIGHTS
AND
MEASURES OF CAPACITY

BATH	KAH
BEKA	LETHECH
COR	LOG
CUBIT	MINA
EPHAH	OMER
GERAH	PIM
HIN	SEAH
HOMER	SHEKEL
ISSARON	TALENT

Who owns the cattle on 1,000 hills?

God. Psalm 50:10

```
L  E  T  H  E  C  H  A  R
E  O  C  O  R  A  B  J  E
K  T  G  B  R  A  N  I  M
E  I  A  E  E  O  C  H  O
H  B  G  L  R  K  T  D  R
S  U  E  A  E  A  A  H  E
F  C  S  H  B  N  P  I  M
K  S  E  A  H  G  T  N  O
I  H  L  K  E  P  H  A  H
```

Word Search 32

BIRTH OF ISAAC

Who was Isaac's mother and why was she called the "mother of nations?" Find out in Genesis 17:15-21, Genesis 18:10-14, and Genesis 21:1-8.

ABRAHAM

BORE SON

CHILD GREW

CONCEIVED

COVENANT

EIGHT DAYS OLD

GREAT FEAST

HUNDRED YEARS OLD

IN THE SPRING

ISAAC

LAUGHTER

MOTHER OF NATIONS

NINETY YEARS OLD

OLD AGE

SARAH

WEANED

WIFE

What was the name of Ruth's sister-in-law?

Orpah. Ruth 1:4

66

```
B N I N E T Y Y E A R S O L D
V F O E Y I M T N C I D K L W
P G F S N A T N A N E V O C D
B I I O E V L E Y X J S M H L
W J N F O R U A P L R U Z B O
M O T H E R O F N A T I O N S
E T H C G D M B E U S D L C Y
O K E S O A F Y Q G H K D H A
N R S I H N D M W H J D A L D
H O P A Z E C R Q T V E G U T
A Y R W R L P E C E S N E B H
R B I D C A A S I R D A R H G
A X N F Z X E I E V T E G J I
S U G C H I L D G R E W C A E
H T S A E F T A E R G D G K A
```

Word Search 33

BIRTH OF JESUS

ANGEL	KING OF THE JEWS
BABE	MANGER
BEAR A SON	MARY
BETROTHED	MYRRH
BORN IN BETHLEHEM	NAZARETH
CHRIST THE LORD	NIGHT
DEATH OF HEROD	NO PLACE IN INN
DREAM	REJOICED
FLEE TO EGYPT	SAVIOR
FLOCK	SHEPHERDS
FRANKINCENSE	SON OF GOD
GIFTS	STAR IN THE EAST
GOLD	SWADDLING CLOTHS
GOOD NEWS	VIRGIN
GREAT JOY	WARNED
HEROD THE KING	WIFE
HOLY SPIRIT	WISE MEN
JESUS	WITH CHILD
JOSEPH	WORSHIP

```
B L H N O P L A C E I N I N N A B E
M O E M A N G E R A C T H G I N W B
C H R I S T T H E L O R D F E G I A
N O O N D G I D O G F O N O S E F B
E L D V I R G I N Y K O J H N L E K
K Y T H W N D L O G C P T J E S U S
I S H P A Q B J L H O O M E C T M D
N P E I R O T E P R L N T D N F Y O
G I K H N A W E T C F O S E I I R R
O R I S E O S I G H E T M C K G R E
F I N R D O S N T G L A U I N O H H
T T G O J M I A Y H E E V O A O N F
H W P W A L U P R R C Y H J R D E O
E V X R D Z T Q D A B H A E F N M H
J R Y D E H T O R T E B I R M E E T
E N A Z A R E T H Y S B W L C W S A
W W R O I V A S H E P H E R D S I E
S T A R I N T H E E A S T Z T X W D
```

Word Search 34

BIRTH OF MOSES

How did Moses become Pharaoh's daughter's son, and why did she name him Moses? Find out in Exodus 2:1-10.

BABE WAS CRYING

BASKET

BATHE AT THE RIVER

BITUMEN AND PITCH

BULRUSHES

FETCH

GOODLY CHILD

HEBREW

HID THREE MONTHS

HOUSE OF LEVI

NURSE

PHARAOH'S DAUGHTER

REEDS

RIVER'S BRINK

SENT MAID

SISTER

TOOK PITY ON HIM

WAGES

Who succeeded Solomon as King of Israel?

Rehoboam, his son. 2 Chronicles 9:31

70

```
S H T N O M E E R H T D I H K R
U T S Q D I A M T N E S G M E E
R W O Y A E V C G I K N O T D V
M I S O U Q R E T S I S H O L I
W C V Y K E K F L Y M G I A I R
S O U E Q P W A R F U C Y S H E
E G T K R E I C M A O W I E C H
H O E Q U S S T D S A E W S Y T
S X K Z C A B S Y G B R S R L T
U V S A W T H R E O R B N U D A
R F A E J O L S I P N E H N O E
L N B T A X B D Z N V H R P O H
U A V R X B F J L H K D I Z G T
B Z A B F J N P T R L H D M X A
V H C T I P D N A N E M U T I B
P T R E E D S P N R F E T C H L
```

Word Search 35

BOOKS OF THE BIBLE BY CATEGORY
(in the order they appear in the Bible)

THE LAW

HISTORY (OLD TESTAMENT)

POETRY

MAJOR PROPHETS

MINOR PROPHETS

THE GOSPELS

HISTORY (NEW TESTAMENT)

PAULINE LETTERS

GENERAL LETTERS

PROPHECY

Recite Hezekiah 3:17.

Hezekiah was a king, not a book.

72

```
P  O  E  T  R  Y  E  K  O  M  I  G  A  G
R  A  C  Q  W  S  A  E  C  Y  S  U  S  E
O  I  U  H  I  S  T  O  R  Y  L  T  G  N
P  Q  M  L  U  Y  C  A  W  S  E  O  K  E
H  E  S  G  I  K  O  U  Q  H  P  M  I  R
E  I  Y  C  K  N  G  I  P  E  S  A  W  A
C  O  S  Q  S  U  E  O  Y  A  O  W  M  L
Y  L  N  T  V  X  R  L  Z  T  G  R  P  L
V  B  F  J  O  P  H  D  E  Z  E  X  T  E
B  H  L  F  R  R  N  R  P  T  H  J  D  T
L  P  T  O  X  Z  Y  V  R  N  T  J  H  T
D  B  J  T  H  E  L  A  W  F  Z  E  X  E
B  A  F  J  N  R  V  T  P  L  H  D  R  R
M  I  N  O  R  P  R  O  P  H  E  T  S  S
```

Word Search 36

BOOKS OF THE NEW TESTAMENT
(in the order they appear in the Bible)

MATTHEW

MARK

LUKE

JOHN

ACTS

ROMANS

CORINTHIANS (1&2)

GALATIANS

EPHESIANS

PHILIPPIANS

COLOSSIANS

THESSALONIANS (1&2)

TIMOTHY (1&2)

TITUS

PHILEMON

HEBREWS

JAMES

PETER (1&2)

JOHN (1, 2 &3)

JUDE

REVELATION

```
T I M O T H Y N T P R E T E P
Z H F H I W V B R D X N H O J
E J E N T R E V T P O L P P A
P A G S U E C H K I M O H I M
H Q S W S Y U A T E C I I G E
E J N T L A P A R T L V L Y S
S N A I T A L A G E A E I G N
I A H Z J E M O M S C M P I A
A W D F V L B O N O K N P X I
N K Q E M J N A S I M O I U S
S J R B U D M F L H A Z A X S
R O T D V O N P L U R N N J O
B H E B R E W S D F K H S U L
Y N A E C Q A C T S Q E K G O
S U W O S N A I H T N I R O C
```

Word Search 37

BOOKS OF THE OLD TESTAMENT
(in the order they appear in the Bible)

GENESIS	SONG OF SOLOMON
EXODUS	ISAIAH
LEVITICUS	JEREMIAH
NUMBERS	LAMENTATIONS
DEUTERONOMY	EZEKIEL
JOSHUA	DANIEL
JUDGES	HOSEA
RUTH	JOEL
SAMUEL (1&2)	AMOS
KINGS (1&2)	OBADIAH
CHRONICLES (1&2)	JONAH
EZRA	MICAH
NEHEMIAH	NAHUM
ESTHER	HABAKKUK
JOB	ZEPHANIAH
PSALMS	HAGGAI
PROVERBS	ZECHARIAH
ECCLESIASTES	MALACHI

```
S E T S A I S E L C C E B F K D J
E O B A D I A H I E Z E K I E L O
L R N C G E M I C A H U N H K J E
C U L G E N E S I S K G R N T P L
I T O J O B M Q S K S S U D O X E
N H T X C F V H A I N A H P E Z A
O J U D G E S B D O S U A R W E Y
R B I Y F G A O I E R Z I O N C M
H A H K C H E T L M E F M V A H O
C D C S M L A S P O B J E E H A N
S H A G L T M I E H M B H R U R O
A O L T N X O J M V U O E B M I R
M S A E W Z S O Y E N H N S U A E
U E M R E H T S E H R L A N J H T
E A I S A I A H K M L E I N A D U
L E V I T I C U S I A G J E O C E
D I H I A G G A H B E Z R A F J D
```

Word Search 38

BURNING BUSH

Find out what happened to Moses when he came to Horeb, the mountain of God in Exodus 3:1-15.

AFFLICTION OF PEOPLE

AFRAID

ANGEL

BRING FORTH

BURNING

DELIVER

EGYPT

FATHER-IN-LAW

FLAME OF FIRE

FLOCK

GOOD AND BROAD LAND

HID HIS FACE

HOLY GROUND

HOREB

"I AM WHO I AM"

JETHRO

MIDST OF A BUSH

MILK AND HONEY

MOSES

MOUNTAIN OF GOD

PUT OFF SHOES

SEND TO PHARAOH

SIGN

SUFFERING

WEST SIDE

WILDERNESS

```
A L N H S U B A F O T S D I M P S R
F F A T H E R I N L A W Q T O E V E
R U F R W O Y A E G I C O M U D F V
A H O L Y G R O U N D X D B N I Z I
I M H N I T P E B W L H R A T S J L
D I K U M C Q X B U T O L S A T V E
G L A O R H T E J R R D C N I S F D
N K D G K J H I O E A N G B N E E I
I A L S O R V F O O T E I N O W R H
R N P S U X G M R N L S W N F Q I I
E D Y E A N E B S M O S E S G C F D
F H D N I B D G I J H F I F O Z F H
F O T R W N B H G D V E P Y D A O I
U N B E A G U C N K J X F E I Z E S
S E N D T O P H A R A O H L O N M F
O Y O L M S E O H S F F O T U P A A
T O P I A M W H O I A M W V Y R L C
G S X W Z E G Y P T U Q K C O L F E
```

Word Search 39

CAIN AND ABEL

Find out why Cain killed his brother Abel in
Genesis 4:1-16.

ADAM

"AM I MY BROTHER'S KEEPER?"

ANGRY

BLOOD

CAIN KILLED ABEL

COUNTENANCE FELL

CRYING

CURSED

EAST OF EDEN

EVE

FIELD

FIRSTLINGS OF FLOCK

FUGITIVE

KEEPER OF SHEEP

LAND OF NOD

NO REGARD FOR CAIN

OFFERING OF FRUIT

PUNISHMENT

REGARD FOR ABEL

SEVENFOLD

TILLER OF THE GROUND

TWO BROTHERS

VENGEANCE

WANDERER

```
T N M L L E F E C N A N E T N U O C R
I I B P T W A Y R E V E N X B Z V E S
U A L E B A R O F D R A G E R O P A K
R C O L A N D O F N O D Q U S E E S C
F R O C E J F P M P E R T I E O E T O
F O D G K R N S Q U G D H K V L H O L
O F U A L C O W G N Y E S K E I S F F
G D X D R V H F I I B R J F N Z F E F
N R M P V E O Y T S E W A Q F W O D O
I A T W O B R O T H E R S R O V R E S
R G Y N C C S E T M E X T Z L E E N G
E E A H K U F O D E J G C M D N P E N
F R D L G O R S B N I N R T P G E Q I
F O R V X B T S U T A Y C O B E E F L
O N W S Y Z F I E L D W D A U A K E T
L S Q M W U R A Y D O T B X V N Z N S
C A I N K I L L E D A B E L M C D P R
B M A D A E P J H M O K D R F E T L I
A N G R Y I N C G Q S E V I T I G U F
```

Word Search 40

CHRISTIAN VIRTUES
AND CHARACTER

CLEANLINESS (2 Corinthians 7:1)
CONSECRATION (Romans 12:1-2)
CONTENTMENT (1 Timothy 6:6)
COURAGE (Psalm 27:14)
DILIGENCE (Romans 12:11)
DUTY (Luke 20:21-25)
ENDURANCE (James 1:12)
FAITH (Romans 1:17)
FRUITFULNESS (John 15:1-8)
GODLINESS (Titus 2:11-14)
HAPPINESS (Matthew 5:3-12)
HOLINESS (1 Peter 1:13-16)
HONOR TO PARENTS (Matthew 15:4)
LOVE (Luke 10:27)
OBEDIENCE (John 14:15-24)
PATIENCE (1 Timothy 6:11)
PEACEFULNESS (John 14:27)
PERSEVERANCE (Romans 12:21)
PURE THINKING (Philemon 4:8)
RESOLUTION (Ephesians 6:10-18)
RIGHTEOUSNESS (Matthew 6:33)
STEDFASTNESS (1 Corinthians 15:58)
STEWARDSHIP (1 Corinthians 4:2)
TEMPERANCE (1 Thessalonians 5:6-8)
TRUST (Psalm 37:3-5)
ZEAL (Titus 2:14)

```
S C E A C O N S E C R A T I O N
T P U R E T H I N K I N G S B D
E F E G A R U O C S G E G S E B
D N F A I T H I S K H C T E D L
F T D H C L A E Z E T N E N I J
A R D U M E N Q C O E E C I E C
S U U N R I F N P R O G N L N O
T S T I L A A U A S U I A N C N
N T Y D T R N P L R S L R A E T
E U O E E F O C T N N I E E C E
S G V P V T U X E W E D V L N N
S Y M A R O C L F G S S E C E T
B E Z O H O L I N E S S S D I M
T H N H A P P I N E S S R J T E
N O I T U L O S E R S K E M A N
H P I H S D R A W E T S P L P T
```

Word Search 41

CHRIST'S THREE TEMPTATIONS

The devil tempted Jesus three times while he was in the wilderness. Find out what happened in Matthew 4:1-11.

ANGELS	MOUNTAIN
BREAD	MOUTH OF GOD
"CAST THYSELF DOWN"	PINNACLE
CHARGE	PROCEEDETH
COMMAND	SATAN
DEVIL	SERVE
FASTED	SON OF GOD
FORTY DAYS	STONES
FORTY NIGHTS	TEMPLE
GLORY	TEMPTED
HANDS	WILDERNESS
HOLY CITY	WORD
JESUS	WORLD
KINGDOMS	WORSHIP
LORD THY GOD	WRITTEN

```
C A E F A S T E D C S U S E J
O A W O R S H I P F T H I G D
M N S R B D O G F O H T U O M
M G J T E M P T E D G L S G N
A E M Y T N A T A S I E E L K
N L O D E H Q V S U N T R O E
D S Y A M R Y E S O Y P V R L
N M T Y P U N S T W T X E Y C
E O I S L R V S E B R E A D A
T D C Y E D E V I L O A E C N
T G Y D G Z S O N O F G O D N
I N L O R D T H Y G O D F B I
R I O D A H T E D E E C O R P
W K H I H A N D S D L R O W G
D R O W C H J M O U N T A I N
```

Word Search 42

CLEANSING OF THE TEMPLE

"It is written, 'My house is the house of prayer': but ye have made it a den of thieves." What were the people doing when Jesus entered the temple in Luke 19:45-46?

ALL THE PEOPLE	SCRIBES
BOUGHT	SOLD
CAST OUT	SOUGHT TO DESTROY
CHIEF PRIESTS	TAUGHT DAILY
DEN OF THIEVES	TEMPLE
HOUSE OF PRAYER	VERY ATTENTIVE
JESUS	

What were the names of Job's three "friends?"

Eliphaz, Bildad, and Zophar. Job 2:11

```
L P R N T A U G H T D A I L Y
E L P O E P E H T L L A S O M
T X H A E G Z J V O C Q R E C
C F B O I U D E H W A T J V Y
H K P W U R M S Y O S T A I B
I S U N Z S L U V E T X Q T S
E S C R I B E S D C O F H N O
F D J G L I N O E O U M K E L
P B O U G H T P F U T W R T D
R T V Y Q T E A Z P C S B T X
I H D O H M L J S F R P L A V
E K I G E Q P N U W R A G Y T
S A U X I C M O H E L Z Y R G
T O F B J N E Y D K R P M E Q
S E V E I H T F O N E D S V R
```

Word Search 43

COINS OF THE BIBLE

ASSARION	LEPTON
AUREUS	MITE
BEKA	MONEY
DARIC	PENNY
DENARIUS	POUND
DRACHMA	SHEKEL
DRAM	SILVER
GERAH	SILVERLINGS
GOLD	TALENT

"An eye for an eye" was an Old Testament rule of punishment. What was Jesus' rule for responding to an offense?

Turn the other cheek. Matthew 5:38-39

```
P  O  R  D  E  N  A  R  I  U  S
E  A  D  Q  A  K  E  B  P  G  I
N  M  S  F  D  R  A  M  N  E  L
N  H  O  S  I  H  I  I  L  G  V
Y  C  L  N  A  T  L  C  E  J  E
A  A  K  O  E  R  N  Q  P  M  R
U  R  P  S  E  Y  I  U  T  R  H
R  D  T  V  X  W  V  O  O  U  A
E  A  L  Y  T  A  L  E  N  T  R
U  I  C  P  O  U  N  D  B  Z  E
S  H  E  K  E  L  E  D  L  O  G
```

Word Search 44

COVENANT OF THE RAINBOW

Read all about the first rainbow in Genesis 9:8-17.

ARK

BIRDS

BOW IN THE CLOUD

CATTLE

COVENANT

DESCENDANTS

DESTROY

EARTH

ESTABLISH

EVERLASTING

FLOOD

FUTURE

GENERATIONS

GOD

NEVER AGAIN

NOAH

SIGN

SONS

Jonah wasn't the only one sent to Nineveh. What other prophet ministered there?

Nahum. Nahum 1:1

A	D	N	E	V	E	R	A	G	A	I	N	D
G	E	E	C	E	H	N	J	L	G	D	U	B
N	S	F	S	D	R	I	B	M	I	O	D	K
I	T	O	U	C	X	Q	W	T	L	O	A	V
T	R	S	E	R	E	E	C	C	P	L	R	S
S	O	N	A	B	R	N	E	A	Y	F	K	T
A	Y	O	R	U	A	H	D	Z	T	D	C	N
L	E	S	T	I	T	N	O	A	H	T	G	A
R	H	U	H	N	M	K	F	L	N	J	L	N
E	F	N	I	H	S	I	L	B	A	T	S	E
V	X	W	A	Z	V	S	I	G	N	O	S	V
E	O	B	D	O	G	E	W	F	D	Y	C	O
B	G	E	N	E	R	A	T	I	O	N	S	C

Word Search 45

CREATION

Read all about God's great creation in Genesis 1.

BEASTS (of the earth)	MAN
BIRDS	MOON
CATTLE	NIGHT
CREEPING (things)	SEAS
DAY	STARS
EARTH	SUN
FISH	VEGETATION
HEAVEN	WOMAN
LIGHT	

Elijah didn't die, as you know. Who else was "taken away?"

Enoch, Methuselah's dad. Genesis 5:21-24

```
H  E  A  V  E  N  O  O  M  A  E
T  C  G  C  R  E  E  P  I  N  G
R  K  Q  A  O  S  I  M  O  U  H
A  U  C  T  Y  E  A  I  G  S  W
E  D  H  T  L  N  T  N  I  R  J
O  A  Q  L  H  A  A  F  M  P  T
K  Y  I  E  T  G  S  M  A  N  S
X  B  F  E  Z  D  I  V  O  E  T
L  I  G  H  T  T  J  N  A  W  A
D  E  H  L  R  N  P  S  F  B  R
V  S  D  R  I  B  E  A  S  T  S
```

Word Search 46

CRUCIFIXION

Who carried Jesus' cross to Golgotha and what does "Golgotha" mean? Find out in Matthew 27:32-33.

ACCUSED	MURDER
BODY OF JESUS	NO ANSWER
CAST LOTS	PILATE
CENTURION	PUT TO DEATH
CHIEF PRIESTS	QUESTIONED
CONTEMPT	RELEASED BARABBAS
CRIME	SCRIBES
CROSS	SENT TO HEROD
CRUCIFY	SIMON OF CYRENE
DARKNESS	SIXTH HOUR
GAVE SENTENCE	SOLDIERS
GORGEOUS APPAREL	THE SKULL
JOSEPH	TOMB
KING OF THE JEWS	TWO CRIMINALS
LINEN SHROUD	VINEGAR
MOCKED	WRAPPED
MULTITUDES	

```
G Z G C A S T L O T S N A T G N Q H
A O P I L A T E H T A E D O T T U P
V M R K I N G O F T H E J E W S E E
E S S G D E P P A R W Z F S A I S S
S L E C E N T U R I O N Y B X M T O
E A N E T O L P Y E R F B M S O I J
N N T L R S U E M U D A S O V N O W
T I T N O A N S W E R R L R S O N S
E M O K E B G D A A T D U S E F E U
N I H D Q M K E B P I N O M B C D S
C R E A D O I D N E P R O O I Y T E
E C R R Q T E R R I C A X C R R H J
K O O K C S P S C W V J R K C E E F
C W D N A M U L T I T U D E S N S O
S T S E I R P F E I H C I D L E K Y
V B L S I P B L I N E N S H R O U D
J E O S C R U C I F Y U A H O A L O
R U O H H T X I S A C C U S E D L B
```

Word Search 47

DANIEL IN THE LIONS' DEN

Find out what happened to Daniel when he was thrown into a den of lions in Daniel 6.

AGREEMENT	KINGDOM
COMPLAINT	NO ERROR OR FAULT
COUNSELORS	ORDINANCE
DANIEL	PALACE
DEN OF LIONS	PETITION
DISTRESSED	PRAYED
EXCELLENT SPIRIT	SATRAPS
FAITHFUL	SHUT LIONS' MOUTHS
FASTING	SIGN DOCUMENT
FOUND BLAMELESS	SIGNET
GOD SENT ANGEL	STONE
GOVERNORS	THIRTY DAYS
INTERDICT	THREE PRESIDENTS
KING DARIUS	THREE TIMES A DAY
	TONE OF ANGUISH

```
T B E T H R E E P R E S I D E N T S
T H I R T Y D A Y S D G L S I C H S
A G R E E M E N T D E Y A R P U F E
T O N E O F A N G U I S H O T H J L
I V O D E S S E R T S I D L N M R E
R E I K S T O N E N S A I E I X T M
I R T I O G I Q U W N O L S A V P A
P N I N Y O A M D I N H U N L T F L
S O T G B D E I E S G C F U P C Z B
T R E D M S O L M S Q J H O M I L D
N S P A K E S O R N A P T C O D T N
E A A R T N U Z B A W D I Y C R E U
L T L I V T U O R D I N A N C E N O
L R A U H A G N I T S A F Y X T G F
E A C S C N E I M K G M O D G N I K
C P E S I G N D O C U M E N T I S D
X S F H D E N O F L I O N S J N P L
E O R Q T L U A F R O R O R R E O N
```

Word Search 48

DAVID AND GOLIATH

Who was Goliath and why did David kill him? Find out in 1 Samuel 17:4-51.

ANGER

ARMY

COAT OF MAIL

CUT OFF HEAD

DAVID

DISMAYED

DRAW FOR BATTLE

ELIAB

ENCAMPMENT

FELL TO GROUND

FIVE SMOOTH STONES

FOREHEAD

GATH

GOLIATH

GREATLY AFRAID

GREAVES

GREETED BROTHERS

HEIGHT

HELMET OF BRONZE

JAVELIN

KILLED

LEGS

NAME OF THE LORD

PHILISTINE

RAN TO THE RANKS

SERVANTS OF SAUL

SHEEP

SHEPHERD'S BAG

SHIELD BEARER

SHOULDERS

SIX CUBITS AND A SPAN

SLING

SON OF JESSE

SPEAR

STAFF

STOOD AND SHOUTED

STRUCK

WEAVER'S BEAM

YOUNGEST

```
H L P R N F I V E S M O O T H S T O N E S
E L T T A B R O F W A R D O S N M A Q I R
L S H E P H E R D S B A G W E U M B X Y E
M K E T C X Z A N G E R C M A E D C V P H
E N F R E U T H G I E H P H O L U O J E T
T A W D V G T M I A K M D F N B N A O E O
O R P E D A W O V Z A R T Y I T B T X H R
F E S Y A Q N E F C V H U T L A D O C S B
B H L A E V S T N F E N S D E R G F O R D
R T Q M H P E E S L H A M I V E R M U S E
O O V S E F T R O O N E W V A R E A E X T
N T S I R F Y R S D F B A A J A A I L A E
Z N R D O A D Z A B C S E D F E T L I D E
E A E L F T G S L P E K A S N B L I A G R
J R D E H S P E A R M A Q U R D Y O B O G
T W L G N A Y G A T H A M C L L A V E L D
A X U S N D N U O R G O T L L E F U B I F
R Y O U N G E S T G S L I N G I R I M A K
M P H D E L L I K C U R T S J H A H L T N
Y O S O N O F J E S S E N I T S I L I H P
Q A S B R P D E T U O H S D N A D O O T S
```

Word Search 49

EXAMPLES OF SIN

ADULTERY (Matthew 5:27-32)

ANGER (Matthew 5:22-24)

ANXIETY (Matthew 6:19-34)

CONCEIT (Luke 18:9-14)

COVETOUSNESS (Mark 7:21-23)

CRIME (Matthew 15:17-20)

DECEIT (Matthew 23:27-28)

DEPRAVITY (John 3:19-21)

DIVORCE (Mark 10:2-12)

DRUNKENNESS (Galatians 5:21)

ENVY (Proverbs 14:30)

EXCUSES (Luke 14:15-24)

EXTRAVAGANCE (1 Timothy 6:7-12)

FALSE CONFIDENCE (Matthew 7:24-27)

FALSEHOOD (Ephesians 4:25)

FAULTFINDING (Matthew 7:1-5)

GOSSIP (Leviticus 19:16)

GREED (Luke 12:15-31)

HATRED (1 John 3:14-15)

INTEMPERANCE (Proverbs 20:1)

JUDGING (Matthew 7:1)

LIP SERVICE (Matthew 7:21-23)

LUST (Matthew 5:28; Romans 1:27)

PRIDE (Mark 7:22)

REVENGE (Matthew 5:43-48)

SELF-EXALTATION (Luke 14:11)

SELF-RIGHTEOUSNESS (Luke 18:11-14)

SWEARING (Leviticus 19:12; Colossians 3:8)

WORLDLINESS (1 John 2:15-17)

```
M R P N O I T A T L A X E F L E S
F E M I R C U G N E X C U S E S O
F A L S E C O N F I D E N C E F Q
T S U L W S O Y J U D G I N G A V
W E A L S E T V D Y D E S B D L S
I C X I T E A E E G U Z U H S D
W N P M I F E R R T O K L O E E P
O A T X L R I T I E O T J N N H E
R G N E G Q A N T N E U N S D O C
L A T D M H R H D R G E S E U O I
D V V I Z P G R Y I K X P N N D V
L A C R A I E B W N N R D C E Y R
I R E P R V H R U J A G E G M S E
N T I F E F L R A V N I P K Q O S
E X L N G R D T I N T I E C E D P
S E G P N S W T V E C R O V I D I
S E Q B A Z Y Q I S R E E N V Y L
```

Word Search 50

FAMINE IN GILGAL

"O man of God, there is death in the pot!" Find out what was really in the pot in 2 Kings 4:38-44.

A HUNDRED MEN	HAVE SOME LEFT
BOIL POTTAGE	LOAVES OF BARLEY
DEATH IN THE POT	MAN FROM BAALSHALISHAH
ELISHA	MEAL
FAMINE	NO HARM
FIELD	POURED
FIRST FRUITS	SACK
FRESH EARS OF GRAIN	SERVANT
GATHER HERBS	SONS OF PROPHETS
GILGAL	"THEY SHALL EAT"
GOURDS	WILD VINE
GREAT POT	WORD OF THE LORD

```
H D E A T H I N T H E P O T M Q U W O S
V A P T Z X M R N E N I V D L I W Y T A
B F H J D B N R E H Q K O T S V L R N S
G S C S T O P T A E R G L A U I O M A P
V A D T I I Y C G H I X C L D N A K V N
S Z E R H L U F E W O K B L I D V J R M
T M V R U P A B L O Y N Q A T R E C E F
E S Z N W O X H I A P U R G D O S A S H
H G M Q W T G I S O R G T L K L O H V A
P N X H Y T Z P H L F J S I U E F U L V
O E N I M A F B A O A F D G I H B N O E
R K E M L G H N S C G A P J L T A D P S
P Q V A B E G R S X D O B Z U F R R H O
F A E R W C A E I F U T Y M D O L E J M
O M K M R E U P W R S V T L O D E D O E
S G A T H E R H E R B S E N L R Y M Q L
N R V S Z C E D B X T I L H Y O F E K E
O A E G S W F I N D F M P U Q W J N O F
S R B F J H L D T H E Y S H A L L E A T
F I R S T F R U I T S I C G M K E T P M
```

Word Search 51

FOR WHAT SIN SHALL NO MAN
BE FORGIVEN?

Locate and loop only the words underlined in this verse found in Luke 12:10 (KJV).

"And whosoever shall speak a word against the Son of man, it shall be forgiven him: but unto him that blasphemeth against the Holy Ghost it shall not be forgiven."

BONUS BIBLE TRIVIA

People weren't given permission to eat meat until after the flood. Genesis 9:3

B	F	E	S	P	E	A	K	I	D	H
H	S	O	N	O	F	M	A	N	T	O
F	L	J	R	N	G	M	K	E	C	L
U	O	V	E	G	X	Q	M	U	S	Y
R	N	T	V	W	I	E	Y	H	P	G
A	S	I	E	C	H	V	G	I	Z	H
F	H	D	O	P	B	H	E	M	E	O
L	A	I	S	O	S	M	Q	N	K	S
J	L	A	O	A	G	A	I	N	S	T
P	L	N	H	V	T	X	R	D	B	E
B	U	Z	W	O	R	D	A	C	W	Y

Word Search 52

GOD TESTS ABRAHAM

Read all about Abraham and his son Isaac and what happened when they went to the land of Moriah in Genesis 22:1-19.

ABRAHAM	MULTIPLY
ANGEL	NATIONS
BLESS	OBEYED
BOUND ISAAC	OFFER
BUILT ALTAR	POSSESS
BURNT OFFERING	RAM
CUT WOOD	ROSE EARLY
DESCENDANTS	SECOND TIME
ENEMIES	SLAY
FEAR GOD	SON
FIRE	SWORN
GATE	TESTED
HAND	"THE LORD WILL PROVIDE"
HORNS	THICKET
KNIFE	THIRD DAY
LAND OF MORIAH	TWO YOUNG MEN
LIFTED UP EYES	"WHERE IS THE LAMB?"
LOVE	WORSHIP
MOUNTAIN	

```
E  S  T  N  A  D  N  E  C  S  E  D  A  F  N  Y  C  O
M  D  O  O  W  T  U  C  D  E  H  D  O  G  R  A  E  F
I  L  I  F  T  E  D  U  P  E  Y  E  S  B  O  D  G  F
T  I  F  V  X  L  O  N  O  S  Q  Y  T  A  W  D  A  E
D  P  I  R  O  S  J  W  K  N  I  F  E  B  S  R  M  R
N  C  R  K  V  R  Z  N  S  U  R  B  M  R  C  I  L  D
O  A  E  L  G  E  P  S  J  A  K  A  G  A  Y  H  A  P
C  A  H  A  N  G  E  L  T  F  L  N  A  H  L  T  N  S
E  S  B  I  R  S  M  L  L  E  O  R  T  A  P  H  D  Q
S  I  T  L  S  O  A  X  H  I  A  W  E  M  I  A  O  C
V  D  Y  O  E  T  S  T  U  Z  W  V  B  M  T  N  F  D
P  N  P  E  L  S  S  E  I  G  O  D  K  A  L  D  M  T
I  U  H  I  F  I  S  J  E  L  M  L  R  R  U  E  O  E
H  O  U  N  E  O  P  N  I  A  T  N  U  O  M  T  R  K
S  B  U  R  N  T  O  F  F  E  R  I  N  G  L  S  I  C
R  S  E  I  M  E  N  E  Q  Y  A  L  S  U  S  E  A  I
O  H  O  R  N  S  R  V  T  O  B  E  Y  E  D  T  H  H
W  S  N  O  I  T  A  N  E  M  G  N  U  O  Y  O  W  T
```

Word Search 53

GOOD SAMARITAN

Find out what happened to the man who "fell among robbers" in Luke 10:29-37.

BEAT	ONE WHO SHOWED MERCY
BOUND UP WOUNDS	PASSED BY ON OTHER SIDE
BROUGHT TO INN	POURED ON OIL AND WINE
COMPASSION	PRIEST
FELL AMONG ROBBERS	PROVED NEIGHBOR
INNKEEPER	SAMARITAN
JERICHO	SET ON OWN BEAST
JERUSALEM	STRIPPED
LEVITE	TWO DENARII

BONUS BIBLE TRIVIA

Locusts, katydids, crickets, and grasshoppers were considered clean food for the Israelites. What's for lunch? Leviticus 11:22

```
P O U R E D O N O I L A N D W I N E B
N A T I R A M A S C K G V O T E M I Q
F L S F J D H N N I O T T H G U O R B
E N I S W R A G S E P C U Y J K H D C
L X I R E P E E K N N I B F Z I D E L
L O R L S D X N B V D Q F Y K H A P B
A P A M R O B H G I E N D E V O R P O
M T N C E G R Y J W L U I Z O R M I U
O N E W H O S H O W E D M E R C Y R N
N S D N U P A Q Y N C N E K W J M T D
G X O B Z F I T D G O V L H P O N S U
R G W Q A W N I C I S T Y K E P U L P
O V T H M B R X S O J D H T Z R F P W
B U Q J E R U S A L E M J E R I C H O
B F V Y R W A H O A J E L S R E R C U
E N G T X P I T Z P K B Q T D S M S N
R B A E M I G P L N D J H Q O T I N D
S E T O N O W N B E A S T C K F M D S
B V C R B U D A E C S R T L E V I T E
```

Word Search 54

ISAAC AND REBEKAH

Find out how and why Rebekah was chosen to be the wife of Isaac in Genesis 24.

ABRAHAM
AROSE IN THE MORNING
BLESSED IN ALL THINGS
BORN TO BETHUEL
BROTHER LABAN
CHOICE GIFTS
CITY OF NAHOR
COSTLY ORNAMENTS
COVERED HERSELF
DEPARTED
DRINK
FATHER'S HOUSE
FOOD
GOLD RING
HE LOVED HER
ISAAC
JAR
LIFTED UP EYES
LODGE
MAIDEN
MEDITATE IN THE FIELD

MESOPOTAMIA
RAIMENT
REBEKAH
SERVANT
SHOULDER
SILVER AND GOLD
SPENT THE NIGHT
SPRING
STEDFAST LOVE
TAKE A WIFE
TEN CAMELS
TENT
TIME OF EVENING
TROUGH
TWO BRACELETS
VEIL
VERY FAIR
VIRGIN
WATER CAMELS
WELL OF WATER

```
M T N A V R E S P E N T T H E N I G H T
S E Y E P U D E T F I L O D G E B E G I
D F D A C E E V O L T S A F D E T S U M
C H O I C E G I F T S S P R I N G T O E
J G I M T A K E A W I F E N R N O N R O
A J N A E A H R E B E K A H I K L E T F
R B E T N R T L S P R B O H A S D M R E
E O D O C A M E Q T A N T I F H R A E V
S R I P A I C S I L E L V S Y O I N T E
U N A O M M U I R N L L T A R U N R A N
O T M S E E W E T A T N E A E L G O W I
H O A E L N H X N Y Z H I C V D A Y F N
S B H M S T L I E V O Y E G A E B L O G
R E A F O O D C F H J F E F R R G T L I
E T R R D E P A R T E D N D I I B S L T
H H B K S L E M A C R E T A W E V O E N
T U A S L R E H D E V O L E H N L C W E
A E E P O S I L V E R A N D G O L D M T
F L E S R E H D E R E V O C Q D R I N K
B G N I N R O M E H T N I E S O R A S R
```

Word Search 55

JACOB'S TWELVE SONS

ASHER

BENJAMIN

DAN

GAD

ISSACHAR

JOSEPH

JUDAH

LEVI

NAPHTALI

REUBEN

SIMEON

ZEBULUN

BONUS BIBLE TRIVIA

King Ahab disguised himself in a battle so the enemy wouldn't try to kill him, but a random arrow hit him anyway. 1 Kings 22:29-35

S	I	M	E	O	N	L	P	J
R	A	H	C	A	S	S	I	O
Z	E	Q	J	T	N	L	V	S
E	R	U	I	U	A	B	R	E
B	Z	V	B	T	D	E	U	P
U	E	W	H	E	H	A	C	H
L	S	P	X	S	N	G	H	O
U	A	M	A	D	A	N	A	Y
N	I	M	A	J	N	E	B	D

Word Search 56

JESUS IN THE TEMPLE

Find out what Jesus said to his mother and father when they found him in the temple in Luke 2:43-52.

AMAZED	QUESTIONS
ANSWERS	STATURE
ASTONISHED	SUBJECT
DOCTORS	TARRIED
"FATHER'S BUSINESS"	TEMPLE
HEARING	THREE DAYS
JERUSALEM	TWELVE YEARS OLD
JESUS	UNDERSTANDING
JOSEPH	WISDOM
MOTHER	
NAZARETH	

BONUS BIBLE TRIVIA

The disciples were first called Christians in Antioch. Acts 11:26

```
F C E K A S T O N I S H E D J
G A L I Q P S M T E M P L E F
N M T C E J B U S D R O H G O
T A Y H P E S O J A S V N N B
W Z A J E S U S U R Y I C I Z
S E S N X R A D A F D M M R C
Y D T B S E S E G N H O E A Q
A I A M P W Y B A K T D L E U
D N T O J E E T U H L S A H E
E Q U T V Z S R E S U I S W S
E S R L X R V R S R I W U Y T
R A E D E I R R A T C N R E I
H W F D B N R D J G V P E L O
T H N A Z A R E T H W U J S N
Q U O K T M S I D O C T O R S
```

Word Search 57

JESUS' UNANSWERABLE QUESTION

Locate and loop only the words underlined in these verses found in Matthew 22:41-46 (KJV).

"While the Pharisees were gathered together, Jesus asked them, Saying, What think ye of Christ? whose son is he?

They say unto him, The son of David.

He saith unto them, How then doth David in spirit call him Lord, saying, The Lord said unto my Lord, Sit thou on my right hand, till I make thine enemies thy footstool?

If David then call him Lord, how is he his son?

And no man was able to answer him a word, neither durst any man from that day forth ask him any more questions."

```
I S T L G A T H E R E D N
H T I A S O M G N I Y A S
T P S K R E H T E G O T R
R T E A B L E Q T H I N K
O D Q S F O O T S T O O L
F U S U A R N E Z H C W L
X B O S E D E V S A I D A
N T N E Y S I E D N T R C
O S F J I J T V L D I O I
M I M R K M H I A G R W U
A R A N S W E R O D I H N
N H K O T S R U D N P N T
P C E P E N E M I E S Q O
```

Word Search 58

JEZEBEL

Who was Naboth and why was he stoned to death? Find out in 1 Kings 21.

AHAB

BLOOD

CHARGE

DOGS

EAT NO FOOD

ELDERS

ELIJAH

EVIL

FASTED

HUMBLED

JEZEBEL

KING OF SAMARIA

NABOTH

NOBLES

PALACE

RENT CLOTHES

SACKCLOTH

SHE WROTE LETTERS

STONE TO DEATH

SULLEN

TAKE POSSESSION

"THE LORD FORBID"

TWO BASE FELLOWS

VALUE IN MONEY

VEGETABLE GARDEN

VEXED

VINEYARD

```
V T H E L O R D F O R B I D A G D
K E C A L A P E H C D K Y F J S I
I B G L N B L E B E Z E J R R T M
N D N E Q A A D T Y N O Z E T O B
G S O P T H W S E O R V T N X N J
O D B O C A A E M X H T A T F E R
F R L H F F B N B G E I D C J T A
S A E A K O I L N L P V O L Q O S
A Y S J M E N N E L L U S O L D K
M E R I I W Z T V G T E S T H E J
A M U L X A O Y A S A G G H T A D
R O A E S R E D L E B R O E O T E
I V C F W B L O O D G A D S B H L
A E I E V I L M O H J H K E A D B
L P H T O L C K C A S C N R N Q M
U S W O L L E F E S A B O W T S U
T A K E P O S S E S S I O N V T H
```

Word Search 59

JOB

What did Job do when he found out his sons and daughters had been killed? Find out in Job 1-42.

APPOINTMENT

BILDAD

BLAMELESS

BLESSED LATTER DAYS

BULLS

BURNT OFFERINGS

CAMELS

CHALDEANS

ELIHU BECAME ANGRY

ELIPHAZ

FEARED GOD

GREAT WIND

LAND OF UZ

LOATHSOME SORES

MESSENGER TO JOB

MONEY

OXEN

PRAYED FOR FRIENDS

RAMS

RENT HIS ROBE

RESTORED FORTUNES

RING OF GOLD

SABEANS

SATAN

SERVANTS

SEVEN SONS

SHAVED HIS HEAD

SHEEP

SLEW

STRUCK HOUSE

SUFFERING

THREE DAUGHTERS

THREE FRIENDS

UPRIGHT

WORSHIPED

YOUNG PEOPLE DEAD

ZOPHAR

```
B E L I H U B E C A M E A N G R Y B E L
Y L R E N T H I S R O B E C F Y E N O M
O H E D G H I D A E H S I H D E V A H S
U N P S L R A P P O I N T M E N T J L M
N M E S S E N G E R T O J O B H K S A S
G R O G E E B L A M E L E S S G T N N D
P Q R N V D D E P I H S R O W R H A D N
E X S I E A Z L C U T A M W U E R E O E
O D Y R N U S T A N B E V C P A E D F I
P E L E S G I A A T S F K H R T E L U R
L J K F O H O V B O T H G A I W F A Z F
E Q M F N T R F R E O E H O G I R H A R
D P R U S E N E G U A P R S H N I C H O
E C T S S R S V S O O N W D T D E A P F
A R B E U S D E Y Z L A S X A Z N M I D
D A D L I B F E A R E D G O D Y D E L E
F M C B U R N T O F F E R I N G S L E Y
H S G K J S H E E P D I L E W E L S M A
Q S L L U B N R X U S A T A N P X T V R
R E S T O R E D F O R T U N E S O S W P
```

Word Search 60

JOHN 3:16

This verse has been translated into over 1100 languages. Find 25 of them in the puzzle.

AFRIKAANS	ITALIAN
ARABIC	JAPANESE
CHINESE	KOREAN
DANISH	MALAY
DUTCH	NORWEGIAN
ENGLISH	PORTUGUESE
FINNISH	RUSSIAN
FRENCH	SINHALESE
GERMAN	SPANISH
GREEK	SWEDISH
HEBREW	TAMIL
HINDI	VIETNAMESE
ICELANDIC	

```
V A F R I K A A N S L A O C K
U I Q V N A Y H I N D I S I O
D P E T E S E N A P A J M B R
B A W T F Z H E H K H X C A E
M N N G N A J S M D L I F R A
R A O I L A I E U E H Q I A N
T M L E S D M H S P S V N S C
H R S A E H C E W E I A N Y I
S E V W Y N U Z S B N L I D D
I G S X E G F C H E A I S U N
L I D R U S S I A N P M H T A
G K F T L E O N G J S A M C L
N O R W E G I A N P W T R H E
E O U Q Z X W E R B E H Y S C
P V G R E E K T N A I L A T I
```

Word Search 61

JOHN THE BAPTIST

Read all about the birth, life, and death of John the Baptist and why a woman named Herodias held a grudge against him and wanted him beheaded in Matthew 3, Matthew 14:1-12, Mark 6:14-29, Luke 1:5-80, and Luke 3:1-20.

ANGEL

BANQUET

BAPTISM

BAPTIZED JESUS

BEHEADED

BIRTH

ELIZABETH

FORGIVENESS OF SINS

GARMENT OF CAMEL HAIR

GREW

GRUDGE

HERODIAS DANCED

HEROD'S BIRTHDAY

ISRAEL

JOHN

LEATHER GIRDLE

LOCUSTS

MANIFESTATIONS

MULTITUDES

PHARISEES

PLATTER

PREACHING GOOD NEWS

PRISON

REPENTANCE

RIVER JORDAN

SADDUCEES

SON

STRONG IN SPIRIT

WATER

WILDERNESS

WILD HONEY

ZECHARIAH

```
S T R O N G I N S P I R I T C W S R
N S E E C U D D A S E L E A R S I E
I A W G Y E L D R I G R E H T A E L
S U S E J D E Z I T P A B I H Y U I
F S H S N F O K L J D L B L A A Y Z
O N W I L D H O N E Y Q E M I D U A
S O I W N H O J O H G M H W R H N B
S I L N A Q X O T D A N E B A T A E
E T D E G D U R G C E R A V H R D T
N A E P T M I P F G G I D S C I R H
E T R G K B C O E R N N E T E B O Z
V S N R E T T A L P S I D S Z S J L
I E E B A N Q U E T O J H U Z D R N
G F S R E T A W X T N B H C V O E O
R I S M U L T I T U D E S O A R V S
O N R E P E N T A N C E F L R E I I
F A D E C N A D S A I D O R E H R R
G M S I T P A B D S E E S I R A H P
```

Word Search 62

JONAH AND THE WHALE

Find out how Jonah found himself in the belly of a whale in Jonah 1-2.

BELLY	OFFERED SACRIFICE
CAPTAIN	PAID FARE
CAST LOTS	PRAYED
DRY LAND	PRESENCE OF LORD
FAST ASLEEP	SON OF AMITTAI
FISH	SWALLOW
GREAT WIND	TARSHISH
INNER PART OF SHIP	THREE DAYS AND NIGHTS
JOPPA	THREW JONAH INTO SEA
MADE VOWS	THREW WARES INTO SEA
MARINERS AFRAID	VOMITED
MIGHTY TEMPEST	WENT ON BOARD
NINEVEH	WICKEDNESS

```
O A D R O L F O E C N E S E R P C S
A F A S T A S L E E P D F B P I T O
E I F E M K G S T O L T S A C H S N
S S S E N D E K C I W H I D G S E O
O W J G R E A T W I N D D I L F P F
T O N W Q E V A F X F T N A P O M A
N V W R A O D I B A S D A R U T E M
I E E Y L B S S R C N A L F E R T I
S D N C B H D E A A D Z Y A N A Y T
E A T V M F I F S C H L R S I P T T
R M O O C J M Y E G R K D R A R H A
A P N M N O A P P O J I Q E T E G I
W N B I E D R T X V G S F N P N I D
W U O T E H E V E N I N W I A N M E
E Y A E S W A L L O W A H R C I C Y
R B R D P B E L L Y I P J A R E Z A
H H D E H S I H S R A T D M K G F R
T H R E W J O N A H I N T O S E A P
```

Word Search 63

LAST SUPPER

Find out what happened in the "upper room" in Luke 22:1-38.

APOSTLES	JUDAS ISCARIOT
BETRAY	LAMB
BLOOD	MONEY
BREAD	OFFICERS
CONFERRED	PASSOVER
COVENANT	PETER
CUP	PREPARE
DEATH	PRIESTS
DISCIPLES	REMEMBRANCE
DIVIDE	SACRIFICED
DRINK	SATAN
FEAST	SCRIBES
FRUIT OF THE VINE	TABLE
JESUS	UNLEAVENED BREAD
JOHN	UPPER ROOM
	WOE

```
U N L E A V E N E D B R E A D
P D D T C O N F E R R E D F E
P R R S E N N O G I R J T D C
E I I A B M A L F E H O Y E I
R N N E D T T R V F I H A R F
R K K F S I A O B R I N R A I
O U U C J T S B A M L C T P R
O E E S U S S C L N E K E E C
M R R E A D S M I E O M B R A
D Y Y P V I P U R P W S E P S
E Q Q E S A P O S T L E S R T
A V V A N B Y T N A N E V O C
T D D I X O S E B I R C S C Z
H E E G D I M D H F B L O O D
J N N I V E H T F O T I U R F
```

Word Search 64

LONGEST VERSE IN THE BIBLE

Locate and loop only the words underlined in this verse found in Esther 8:9 (KJV).

"Then were the <u>king's</u> <u>scribes</u> <u>called</u> at that <u>time</u> in the <u>third</u> <u>month</u>, that is, the month <u>Sivan</u>, on the <u>three</u> and <u>twentieth</u> <u>day</u> <u>thereof</u>; and it was <u>written</u> <u>according</u> to all that <u>Mordecai</u> <u>commanded</u> unto the <u>Jews</u>, and to the <u>lieutenants</u>, and the <u>deputies</u> and <u>rulers</u> of the <u>provinces</u> which are from <u>India</u> unto <u>Ethiopia</u>, an <u>hundred</u> <u>twenty</u> and <u>seven</u> provinces, unto every province according to the <u>writing</u> thereof, and unto every <u>people</u> after their <u>language</u>, and to the Jews according to their writing, and according to their language."

```
T H E R E Ö F N T Q T H I R D
H P U A W R Y S R E L U R O A
R V S C R I B E S H T N O M Y
E S E C N I V O R P S D K X Z
E A F O O E K H C J S R I D E
D I G R L M W R I T T E N E B
O A I D N I M Q N S O D G P T
P E R I Y T C A L L E D S U W
N T X N B M N Z N E V E S T G
Y H A G T E M O R D E C A I N
C I H F T W E N T I E T H E I
G O K U I D E N J P L D E S T
M P E O P L E N A V I S W Q I
T I O W R A E Y T U D E Z C R
L A N G U A G E S Y J X V B W
```

Word Search 65

THE LORD'S PRAYER

Locate and loop only the words underlined in these verses found in Matthew 6:9-13 (KJV).

"Our <u>Father</u> which <u>art</u> in <u>heaven</u>, <u>Hallowed</u> be thy <u>name</u>. Thy <u>kingdom</u> come. Thy <u>will</u> be <u>done</u> in <u>earth</u>, as it is in heaven.

<u>Give</u> us this <u>day</u> our <u>daily</u> <u>bread</u>.

And <u>forgive</u> us our <u>debts</u>, as we forgive our <u>debtors</u>.

And <u>lead</u> us not into <u>temptation</u>, but <u>deliver</u> us from <u>evil</u>: For <u>thine</u> is the kingdom, and the <u>power</u>, and the <u>glory</u>, <u>for ever</u>. <u>Amen</u>."

BONUS BIBLE TRIVIA

Job's wife thought he had bad breath. Job 19:17

```
R  E  V  I  L  E  D  C  A  R  T
D  E  B  T  O  R  S  H  K  E  H
A  A  W  Y  R  O  L  G  M  V  I
M  R  E  O  E  D  S  P  O  E  N
E  T  V  V  P  D  T  E  D  R  E
N  H  I  F  A  A  B  V  G  O  I
E  G  G  E  T  I  E  I  N  F  L
V  E  R  I  J  L  D  L  I  N  W
A  B  O  D  A  Y  G  O  K  A  I
E  N  F  A  T  H  E  R  N  M  L
H  A  L  L  O  W  E  D  A  E  L
```

Word Search 66

MAJOR AND MINOR PROPHETS
(in the order they appear in the Bible)

ISAIAH	JONAH
JEREMIAH	MICAH
LAMENTATIONS	NAHUM
EZEKIEL	HABAKKUK
DANIEL	ZEPHANIAH
HOSEA	HAGGAI
JOEL	ZECHARIAH
AMOS	MALACHI
OBADIAH	

BONUS BIBLE TRIVIA

Israelites weren't allowed to eat camels. What a
sacrifice! Well, actually they weren't allowed to
sacrifice them either. Leviticus 11:4 .

```
Z E C H A R I A H L O S
N Q S E I A G G A H N P
A M O S Z V T E C O M R
W A I Y E E S C I U X J
B Z H D P O K T M F E O
E O C J H G A I N R I E
D B A L A T H K E M O L
A A L P N U O M W L N R
N D A E I Q I S A I A H
I I M X A A T A C V H Y
E A Z B H A B A K K U K
L H A N O J E L Q P M D
```

Word Search 67

MIRACLES OF THE LORD

(blind) BARTIMAEUS

(blind man at) BETHESDA

BLIND MAN

(miraculous) CATCH OF FISH

(Syrophenician's) DAUGHTER

DEAF, SPEECHLESS (man)

DEMON-POSSESSED (man)

(man with) DROPSY

EPILEPTIC BOY

FEEDING (of 5,000 people)

(wild man of) GADARA

(woman with) HEMORRHAGE

INFIRM WOMAN

(raising of) JAIRUS'S
  DAUGHTER

(two blind men at) JERICHO

LAME MAN (at Bethesda)

(raising of) LAZARUS

(healing of) LEPER

MALCHUS' EAR

(Peter's) MOTHER-IN-LAW

NOBLEMAN'S SON

PALSIED MAN

(feeding of 4,000) PEOPLE

(walking on the) SEA

(Roman centurion's) SERVANT

(calming of the) STORM

TEN LEPERS

TWO BLIND MEN

(man with) UNCLEAN SPIRIT

(raising of) WIDOW'S SON

(water turned to) WINE

(man with) WITHERED HAND

```
J N O B L E M A N S S O N J B A W M
C A T C H O F F I S H B D E L W I R
E P I L E P T I C B O Y R R I I T O
C A N R L G M J E O R E O I N N H T
I L F H U D N L B A K F P C D E E S
U S I S P S P U E A W R S H M X R S
N I R R T O D S V Q R S Y O A S E E
C E M E E Y U A E A N T R C N E D L
L D W P Z H D G U E B R I F A A H H
E M O E C W N H M G H I O M R K A C
A A M L G I I D J A H L N P A M N E
N N A N D Q N D G U S T V T D E D E
S M N E R I W E O N A M E M A L U P
P X E T L E P E R W Z B D R G C A S
I F Y B T N A V R E S U R A Z A L F
R E O R E T H G U A D S E H T E B A
I W A L N I R E H T O M O G J L H E
T F K I D E S S E S S O P N O M E D
```

Word Search 68

MOST PRECIOUS VERSE

Locate and loop only the words underlined in this verse found in John 3:16 (KJV).

"For God so loved the world, that he gave his only begotten son, that whosoever believeth in him should not perish, but have everlasting life."

BONUS BIBLE TRIVIA

Nahor, Abraham's grandfather's name, means "snorer."

```
P  W  O  R  L  D  S  E  V  A  G
O  T  H  X  Q  A  N  Y  U  N  O
N  B  T  O  V  O  Z  W  I  R  D
L  F  E  B  S  J  G  T  E  K  E
Y  C  V  G  H  O  S  D  L  I  V
R  M  E  P  O  A  E  T  O  U  O
P  S  I  E  L  T  N  V  W  Q  L
L  X  L  R  V  B  T  D  E  F  A
I  C  E  I  E  Y  G  E  Z  R  H
F  V  B  S  I  M  L  O  N  P  K
E  J  S  H  O  U  L  D  N  O  T
```

Word Search 69

Find out what happened to Naomi and her daughter-in-law Ruth, and why Ruth was called a "woman of worth" in Ruth 1-4.

ANOINT

BARLEY HARVEST

BEST CLOTHES

BETHLEHEM

BOAZ TOOK RUTH

BORE SON

CHILION

CONCEPTION

DAUGHTERS-IN-LAW

ELIMELECH

EXCHANGING

FAMINE

FOUND FAVOR

GLEANED IN FIELD

GRACIOUS

HUSBAND DIED

JUDAH

KISSED

MAHLON

MAN OF WEALTH

MARA

MEALTIME

MIDNIGHT

MOAB

MORNING

NAOMI

NURSE

OBED

ORPAH

REDEEMING

RUTH CLUNG TO HER

SANDAL

SHEAVES

SIX MEASURES

SONS DIED

SONS TOOK WIVES

STARTLED

TEN YEARS

THRESHING FLOOR

TOWN WAS STIRRED

TWO SONS

UNCOVERED HIS FEET

WASH

WEPT

WIFE

WOMAN OF WORTH

```
T O W N W A S S T I R R E D N O L H A M
D H T R O W O O N A M O W M B N A O M I
A U R M E A T T I M E L P O A O R P A H
U S E E L I E E L E C H A A R I A Q N O
G B D E S R N N M R O Z U B L T M S O B
H A E S E H O O L C T S E B E P G T S E
T N E M S V D D Y O N D A E Y E R L E D
E D M I W E N N O X E Z F W H C A A R L
R D O D A S K K G I B S H G A N C D O E
S I M N S C U U D F I T N E R O I N B I
I E G I H U S S S H L I F H V C O A F F
N D K G T G E E D A N O A I E H U S O N
L N J H P O E E E R E D O M S O S T U I
A T K T S A W W O L U M Y R T Q R A N D
W W I F E E M M R J X A X V C S A R D E
E O T H V O X X C H A N G I N G E T F N
P S S O N S O O O K W I V E S U Y L A A
T O C A N O N N T D C H I L I O N E V E
W N M E H E H H T E B F A M I N E D O L
U S E B Z R H H O T G N U L C H T U R G
```

Word Search 70

NOAH AND THE ARK

Why did God pick Noah to build the ark? Find out in Genesis 6-8.

ALTAR

BURNT OFFERINGS

CATTLE

COVENANT

CREEPING THINGS

DOOR

DOVE

FIFTY CUBITS

FLOOD

FOOD

FORTY DAYS AND NIGHTS

FOWLS

GOPHER WOOD

HAM

JAPHETH

LOWER STORY

MOUNTAIN OF ARARAT

OLIVE LEAF

PITCH

RAIN

RAINBOW

RAVEN

ROOMS

SECOND STORY

SHEM

SIDES

SIX HUNDRED YEARS OLD

SONS' WIVES

THIRD STORY

THREE HUNDRED CUBITS

TWO OF EVERY SORT

WIFE

WINDOW

```
F O O D A T Y R O T S D R I H T A D
O E L T T A C B D H F J H C B R L O
R A V E N R R U C R G K T I E O T O
T A K S N A W R S E D I S Y S S A W
Y O I T I R O N L E P Q W R G Y R R
D U P N V A D T J H R S A O N R M E
A X F A B F N O A U D E Z T I E C H
Y B E G D O I F P N Y V W S H V Y P
S M O O R N W F H D H I O R T E K O
A N V J M I L E E R F W L E G F I G
N E R U O A V R T E P S I W N O W S
D O O L F T D I H D Q N V O I O T X
N C O V E N A N T C Y O E L P W A D
I E O Z U U O G D U H S L B E T O S
G J F H M O I S K B N C E L E O G L
H P X Y U M E H S I R C A X R V M W
T I S T I B U C Y T F I F S C A B O
S Z T S E C O N D S T O R Y H W A F
```

Word Search 71

OLD TESTAMENT MEN AND WOMEN
OF GREAT FAITH

These men and women are listed in Hebrews 11:4-40.

ABEL	JEPHTHAH
ABRAHAM	JOSEPH
BARAK	MOSES
DAVID	NOAH
ENOCH	RAHAB
GIDEON	SAMSON
ISAAC	SAMUEL
JACOB	SARAH

BONUS BIBLE TRIVIA

When King Xerxes couldn't sleep, he had people
read the record of his reign to him.   Esther 6:1

```
A  L  E  U  M  A  S  B  F  A
S  B  I  D  L  K  A  R  A  B
A  A  R  E  N  O  C  H  G  E
R  H  E  A  H  C  A  J  C  L
A  A  K  M  H  H  S  A  D  N
H  R  P  J  T  A  A  N  A  O
N  O  A  H  A  S  M  O  V  E
U  Q  P  S  I  C  S  W  I  D
S  E  S  O  M  T  O  R  D  I
J  O  S  E  P  H  N  B  V  G
```

Word Search 72

PARABLES OF JESUS

BARREN FIG TREE

DISHONEST STEWARD

FATHER AND TWO SONS

FOUND TREASURE

GOOD SAMARITAN

LABORERS IN VINEYARD

LEAVEN

LOST PIECE OF MONEY

LOST SHEEP

MARRIAGE FEAST

MUSTARD SEED

NET

PHARISEE AND PUBLICAN

POUNDS

PRECIOUS PEARL

PRODIGAL SON

RICH FOOL

RICH MAN AND LAZARUS

SEED

SHEEP AND GOATS

SOWER

TALENTS

TARES

TEN VIRGINS

TWO DEBTORS

UNJUST JUDGE

UNMERCIFUL SERVANT

VINEYARD

WAITING SERVANTS

```
P R E C I O U S P E A R L C F D E E S
F H I L D R I C H F O O L O G S P D I
H T A C J P O U N D S E U K D T R W S
Y M N R H S E R A T S N O E P A O A N
E T E A I M Q N S U D R E N Y O D I O
N W E T V S A H Z T X S B E W G I T S
O O R N U R E N R V D A N V Y D G I O
M D T C V E E E A R F I G A E N A N W
F E G A P I A S A N V D N E S A L G T
O B I H L S R T L N D J E L O P S S D
E T F K U E S G I U D L T I W E O E N
C O N R L U N S I M F P A N E E N R A
E R E P M Q R T R N S I U Z R H O V R
I S R T A E Z C S W S D C B A S X A E
P U R D R A Y E N I V Y B R L R V N H
T E A O U N J U S T J U D G E I U T T
S G B T S A E F E G A I R R A M C S A
O A H F G O O D S A M A R I T A N A F
L D I S H O N E S T S T E W A R D U N
```

Word Search 73

PARTING OF THE RED SEA

Read all about one of the greatest miracles of the Old Testament in Exodus 14.

ANGEL OF GOD

ARMY

CHANGED MIND

CHARIOTS

DEAD UPON SEASHORE

DRY GROUND

EGYPTIANS

ENCAMPED BY SEA

GREAT FEAR

LIFT ROD

MORNING

MOSES

NIGHT PASSED

PEOPLE OF ISRAEL

PHARAOH

PILLAR OF CLOUD

PURSUED

SEA RETURNED

SERVANTS

STRETCH HAND OVER SEA

STRONG EAST WIND

WALL

WATERS DIVIDED

```
D N I W T S A E G N O R T S D M H A
I E W N S Q J V A E Z X K Y R F E E
P H A R A O H G P U L Y T W M S O S
E B T D R Y G R O U N D G D R R I Y
O F E H U C E D O G F O L E G N A B
P J R G R P M Q T V L Y V S X I O D
L N S R Y M O S E S Z O K P U G W E
E A D E G P D N I M D E G N A H C P
O D I A E B T L S N H N C L F T I M
F J V T O R L I A E I L Q I U P N A
I C I F S A K H A N A T P F M A D C
S H D E W V H Y R N E S A T C S E N
R A E A Z C B O F D S W H R X S U E
A R D R T J M U G O B I T O P E S Q
E I D E N R U T E R A E S D R D R H
L O R A L B M C N D O F P G S E U Y
S T N A V R E S V L C S Z X M A P R
S S N W K P I L L A R O F C L O U D
```

Word Search 74

PAULINE LETTERS
(in the order they appear in the Bible)

ROMANS

CORINTHIANS (1&2)

GALATIANS

EPHESIANS

PHILIPPIANS

COLOSSIANS

THESSALONIANS (1&2)

TIMOTHY (1&2)

TITUS

PHILEMON

HEBREWS

BONUS BIBLE TRIVIA

Israelites were forbidden to wear clothes made of two kinds of material. Leviticus 19:19

```
D J C O R I N T H I A N S
H I O S F Q M S P K G N N
G A L A T I A N S T A E A
O T O W N V R A X I U L I
B Y S S H D J M N T F A P
I C S K N L E O Z U M G P
Y N I X R A L R Y S T P I
H S A Q W A I V O A Z U L
T B N F S I K S O D M H I
O J S S E L Q C E P G N H
M R E B X G U F Y H V A P
I H C N O M E L I H P H T
T W D S E Z S W E R B E H
```

Word Search 75

PRODIGAL SON

What did the prodigal son's father do when his son returned home? Find out in Luke 15:11-32.

ANGRY

BEST ROBE

BROTHER

COMPASSION

DANCING

DIVIDED

EAT AND MAKE MERRY

ELDER SON

EMBRACED

FAR COUNTRY

FATHER

FATTED CALF

FEED SWINE

FIELDS

GATHERED

GREAT FAMINE

JOURNEY

KISSED

MUSIC

NO LONGER WORTHY

PODS

RING

SHARE OF PROPERTY

SHOES

SINNED

SPENT EVERYTHING

SQUANDERED

YOUNGER SON

```
E H J O U R N E Y R G N A G S F
G N O L O N G E R W O R T H Y A
N B F D E R E H T A G I O T R T
I R D I B J R O N M Q E R S R H
H O E V C E N L U P S E K D E E
T T R I K O S U O W P D S L M R
Y H E D I T M T C O E V D E E E
R E D E S X A P R C H E E I K N
E R N D S C F P A O R Y N F A I
V B A G E Z F R F S B D N E M W
E I U N D O B K O G S E I U D S
T O Q J E M P N L Q N I S M N D
N O S R E G N U O Y R I O U A E
E D A N C I N G S V C X R N T E
P H Y A T W F L A C D E T T A F
S D O P G R E A T F A M I N E Z
```

153

Word Search 76

PSALM 23 (RSV)

Locate and loop only the words underlined in this psalm.

"The <u>Lord</u> is my <u>shepherd</u>, I shall not <u>want</u>; he <u>makes</u> me lie down in <u>green</u> <u>pastures</u>.

He <u>leads</u> me <u>beside</u> still <u>waters</u>; he <u>restores</u> my <u>soul</u>.

He leads me in <u>paths</u> of <u>righteousness</u> for his name's <u>sake</u>.

Even though I <u>walk</u> through the <u>valley</u> of the <u>shadow</u> of <u>death</u>, I <u>fear</u> no <u>evil</u>; for thou <u>art</u> with me; thy <u>rod</u> and thy <u>staff</u>, they <u>comfort</u> me.

Thou <u>preparest</u> a <u>table</u> before me in the <u>presence</u> of my <u>enemies</u>; thou <u>anointest</u> my <u>head</u> with <u>oil</u>, my <u>cup</u> <u>overflows</u>.

Surely <u>goodness</u> and <u>mercy</u> shall <u>follow</u> me all the <u>days</u> of my <u>life</u>; and I shall <u>dwell</u> in the <u>house</u> of the Lord <u>for ever</u>."

```
R E S T O R E S E R U T S A P
E F I N L H S E M E R C Y R R
V J S L O R D K M O E K G T E
E D I S E B O A F F Q L L R P
R S E T E N E M I E S G I P A
O D A A T N O L Z X R U O V R
F W V F T C S P R E S E N C E
O E Y F G H W U E W O D A H S
L L A Y O D A N O I N T E S T
L L C E O W A L K E I K B G E
O U F L D H F S J L T A B L E
W O M L N R E S H E P H E R D
A S D A E L A Y E T R P G N D
N O S V S Q R A A S A K E I O
T H O U S E T D D V U P U C R
```

Word Search 77

Locate and loop only the words underlined in this last psalm.

"<u>Praise</u> the <u>Lord</u>!

Praise <u>God</u> in his <u>sanctuary</u>; praise him in his <u>mighty</u> <u>firmament</u>!

Praise him for his mighty <u>deeds</u>; praise him <u>according</u> to his <u>exceeding</u> <u>greatness</u>!

Praise him with <u>trumpet</u> <u>sound</u>; praise him with <u>lute</u> and <u>harp</u>!

Praise him with <u>timbrel</u> and <u>dance</u>; praise him with <u>strings</u> and <u>pipe</u>!

Praise him with sounding <u>cymbals</u>; praise him with <u>loud</u> <u>clashing</u> cymbals!

Let <u>everything</u> that <u>breathes</u> praise the Lord!

Praise the Lord!"

E	C	Y	M	B	A	L	S	D	E	E	D
X	V	P	F	H	P	R	A	I	S	E	O
C	L	E	R	B	M	I	T	A	S	M	G
E	I	G	R	A	D	A	N	C	E	I	G
E	T	U	L	Y	H	C	J	L	N	G	N
D	B	R	E	A	T	H	E	S	T	H	I
O	M	L	O	U	D	H	N	K	A	T	D
M	P	D	A	N	O	P	I	P	E	Y	R
G	T	R	U	M	P	E	T	N	R	Q	O
T	Y	O	R	S	T	R	I	N	G	S	C
U	S	L	S	G	N	I	H	S	A	L	C
T	N	E	M	A	M	R	I	F	W	V	A

Word Search 78

QUEEN ESTHER

Find out how and why Esther was made queen in Esther 2:1-18.

ASKED FOR NOTHING	MORNING
BANQUET	NO MOTHER OR FATHER
BEAUTY	OIL OF MYRRH
BEST PLACE IN HAREM	OINTMENTS
CONCUBINES	PALACE
CROWN	PLEASED
CUSTODY OF HEGAI	PORTION OF FOOD
EVENING	PRINCES
FAVOR	REMISSION OF TAXES
FOUND GRACE	SERVANTS
GIFTS	SEVEN CHOSEN MAIDS
GIVEN WHAT SHE DESIRED	SHAASHGAZ
HADASSAH	SPICES
JEW	TENTH MONTH
KING AHASUERUS	THE KING LOVED ESTHER
MADE HER QUEEN	TWELVE MONTHS
MORDECAI ADOPTED HER	VIRGIN

```
R E H D E T P O D A I A C E D R O M D
T W E L V E M O N T H S B A N Q U E T
C H K B E S T P L A C E I N H A R E M
G R E I K M I H R R Y M F O L I O N O
A G O K N I G R I V J L H D S E S O R
S N I W I G N I N E V E O E O C E M N
K P N F N N A T Y W U O D P S A C O I
E H T R T V G H X Q F E R L P R I T N
D A M O Z S B L A F H C A E R G P H G
F S E V E N C H O S E N M A I D S E S
O S N A D H Y N T V U J E S N N E R E
R A T F G T O A K I E E F E C U R O N
N D S L U I H W E J M D R D E O V R I
O A N A T W Q P A L A C E U S F A F B
T H E R N Z A G H S A A H S S O N A U
H B O E R H T N O M H T N E T P T T C
I P V N E E U Q R E H E D A M H S H N
N I C U S T O D Y O F H E G A I E E O
G T S E X A T F O N O I S S I M E R C
```

Word Search 79

QUEEN OF SHEBA

Find out what happened when the Queen of Sheba tested King Solomon in 1 Kings 10:1-13.

"BLESSED BE THE LORD"	NO MORE SPIRIT
BURNT OFFERINGS	OFFICIALS
CAMELS	PRECIOUS STONES
CUPBEARERS	QUEEN OF SHEBA
EXPLAIN	REPORT WAS TRUE
FOOD	RIGHTEOUSNESS
GREAT RETINUE	SERVANTS
HARD QUESTIONS	SPICES
HOUSE	TALENTS OF GOLD
JERUSALEM	TEST
JUSTICE	WISDOM
KING SOLOMON	

```
H M J T A L E N T S O F G O L D
N S S E N O T S S U O I C E R P
S S L N K I N G S O L O M O N S
G E K P O Q I O C N I A L P X E
N N Q E C I T S U J R E C W T C
I S U V S Z T X P A H B A U Y I
R U E F C J W S B T H L M K E P
E O E E U N I T E R T A E R G S
F E N G D T S B A U M I L S P L
F T O T N S D Q R W Q U S O E A
O H F R X E O V E Z B D A Y S I
T G S F S T M I R C J E R H U C
N I H S J E R U S A L E M A O I
R R E P O R T W A S T R U E H F
U L B D S T N A V R E S D O O F
B G A N O M O R E S P I R I T O
```

Word Search 80

RAHAB AND THE SPIES

Read all about Rahab's great courage and faith in Joshua 2:1-22.

BLOOD	MEN WENT OUT
CLOSED	NO COURAGE LEFT
DARK	OATH
DEALT KINDLY	"OUR LIFE FOR YOURS"
DELIVER FROM DEATH	PURSUED
FORDS	RAHAB
GATE	RESPECT
GUILTLESS	ROOF
HARLOT	ROPE
HEARTS MELTED	SAVE FAMILY
HIDE THREE DAYS	SCARLET CORD
HILLS	SPIES
HOUSE	STALKS OF FLAX
JERICHO	STREET
JORDAN	SURE SIGN
JOSHUA	TWO MEN
KING	WINDOW
LODGED	

```
O H C I R E J O S H U A I M K H
S U N O C O U R A G E L E F T I
J D R O C T E L R A C S M A L D
H A R L O T N P U R S U E D X E
H E D O I T W O M E N D N O A T
E S E W F F E P L R M O W O L H
A U A Q I T E T K O U S E L F R
R O L V A N L F R R T N N B F E
T H T G E I D F O C A A T N O E
S T K V U F R O L R X D O G S D
M C I G W E A O W O Y R U I K A
E E N N V B S M Y P A O T S L Y
L P D I Z E S P I E S J U E A S
T S L K D E G D O L T E E R T S
E E Y R A H A B C F Y H G U S E
D R O O F H T A O H I L L S I D
```

Word Search 81

SADDEST VERSE IN THE BIBLE

Locate and loop only the words underlined in this verse found in Mark 15:34 (KJV).

"And at the <u>ninth</u> <u>hour</u> <u>Jesus</u> <u>cried</u> with a <u>loud</u> <u>voice</u>, <u>saying</u>, <u>Eloi</u>, Eloi, <u>lama</u> <u>sabachthani</u>? <u>which is</u>, being <u>interpreted</u>, <u>My God</u>, my God, <u>why</u> hast thou <u>forsaken</u> me?"

BONUS BIBLE TRIVIA

There were 12 baskets full of leftovers when Jesus fed a crowd of people. Matthew 14:20

```
H  T  N  I  N  J  M  E  L  O  I
K  O  F  O  R  S  A  K  E  N  N
S  N  U  T  D  J  R  O  A  L  T
Q  V  Z  R  E  P  A  H  U  Y  E
W  B  X  S  I  E  T  I  C  W  R
H  F  U  E  R  H  G  W  H  D  P
I  S  P  M  C  S  M  H  Q  J  R
C  A  M  A  L  I  K  Y  T  O  E
H  N  B  L  R  U  O  Z  G  V  T
I  A  C  W  D  Y  A  V  X  O  E
S  A  Y  I  N  G  B  L  O  U  D
```

Word Search 82

SAMSON AND DELILAH

What happened to Samson when Delilah had his head shaved? Read all about it in Judges 14-16.

ASHKELON	LION	TORCHES
AVENGED	OLIVE ORCHARDS	TORMENT
BIND	PILLARS	WATER
BOWSTRINGS	PRISON	WEAK
BRONZE FETTERS	RAID	WEAVE
BURIED	RAZOR	WEB
BURNED	RIDDLE	WEPT
DAUGHTER OF PHILISTINE	ROCK OF ETAM	WIFE
DEATH	ROPES	
DELILAH	SAMSON	
ENTICE	SECRET	
FEAST	SEVEN DAYS	
FESTAL GARMENTS	SEVEN LOCKS	
FOXES	SEVENTH DAY	
GAZA	SHAVED	
GAZITES	SILVER	
GRAIN	SLAUGHTER	
HARLOT	SMOTE	
HOLLOW PLACES	SPLIT	
HONEY	STRENGTH	
HOT ANGER	SWARM OF BEES	
JAWBONE	THIRSTY	
KILLED	THIRTY COMPANIONS	
LEHI	TIMNAH	
LINEN GARMENTS	TOMB OF MANOAH	

```
T O M B O F M A N O A H A D R I D D L E
S H L B C S G N I R T S W O B G A Z N H
A O I U E F B S D R A H C R O E V I L O
E T N R D E L I L A H Q O D E A T H Y L
F A E I T H Y A D H T N E V E S S W T L
S N N E O Y E N O H Z I P L I N I K S O
T G G D R J C O S E P O R L M F L E R W
N E A I M A B O F L E H I D E R V N I P
E R R A E I Z E M R I H S E E E E O H L
M E M R N B T O S P P O O L N T R B T A
R T E D T T U R R F A T N L T H D W G C
A A N S E H C R O T U N O I I G E A A E
G W T R V K X R N C P C I K C U G J Z S
L A S H A V E D Z E K E W O E A N W I E
A T Z E J T I L P S D O W E N L E E T T
T I W A H T G N E R T S F L I S V B E O
S M K G R A I N G B S E V E N D A Y S M
E N U P I L L A R S E X O F T E R C E S
F A E V A E W S E E B F O M R A W S C H
D H A R L O T D N O L E K H S A M S O N
```

Word Search 83

SHORTEST CHAPTER IN THE BIBLE

Locate and loop only the words underlined in this 117th psalm (KJV).

"O <u>praise</u> the <u>Lord</u>, all ye <u>nations</u>: praise him, all ye <u>people</u>.

For his <u>merciful</u> <u>kindness</u> is <u>great</u> <u>toward</u> us: and the <u>truth</u> of the Lord <u>endureth</u> for ever. Praise ye the Lord."

BONUS BIBLE TRIVIA

David pretended to be insane once by marking up a door and drooling all over his face. 1 Samuel 21:13

```
E   S   I   A   R   P   K   L   N
D   N   O   L   E   S   U   Q   K
R   P   D   O   M   F   R   T   I
O   T   P   U   I   X   O   T   N
L   L   U   C   R   W   V   R   D
E   W   R   B   A   E   Y   U   N
Z   E   G   R   E   A   T   T   E
M   C   D   H   A   G   E   H   S
D   F   N   A   T   I   O   N   S
```

Word Search 84

SOLOMON'S PRAYER OF DEDICATION

Locate and loop only the words underlined in these verses found in 2 Chronicles 6:41-42 (RSV).

"And now <u>arise</u>, O Lord God, and go to thy <u>resting place</u>, thou and the <u>ark</u> of thy <u>might</u>.

Let thy <u>priests</u>, O Lord God, be <u>clothed</u> with <u>salvation</u>, and let thy <u>saints</u> <u>rejoice</u> in thy <u>goodness</u>.

O Lord God, do not <u>turn</u> <u>away</u> the <u>face</u> of thy <u>anointed</u> one!

<u>Remember</u> thy <u>steadfast</u> <u>love</u> for <u>David</u> thy <u>servant</u>."

BONUS BIBLE TRIVIA

When Asa, King of Judah, was old he got diseased feet. 1 Kings 15:23

```
R  E  M  E  M  B  E  R  L  O  Y
M  P  D  I  V  A  D  M  K  R  A
T  S  D  E  T  N  I  O  N  A  W
S  E  R  E  Q  G  N  O  E  E  A
A  R  S  W  H  U  I  N  C  F  P
F  V  E  T  V  T  R  I  A  T  R
D  A  V  S  A  U  O  C  L  A  I
A  M  O  V  T  J  E  L  P  R  E
E  T  L  X  E  I  B  A  C  I  S
T  A  Z  R  S  T  N  I  A  S  T
S  X  E  N  D  O  O  G  D  E  S
```

Word Search 85

SON OF THE SHUNAMMITE

Find out what happened when Elisha met a wealthy Shunammite woman in 2 Kings 4:8-37.

BED	LAP
BITTER DISTRESS	LAY STAFF UPON CHILD
BORE SON	MOUNT CARMEL
CHAIR	"MY HEAD, MY HEAD!"
CHILD GREW	OPENED EYES
COMMANDER OF ARMY	PRAYED
CONCEIVED	ROOF CHAMBER
EAT SOME FOOD	SADDLED THE ASS
ELISHA	SERVANT
FEET	SHE HAD NO SON
FLESH BECAME WARM	SHUNEM
GEHAZI	SNEEZED SEVEN TIMES
HE DIED	SPRING
HOLY MAN	STOOD IN DOORWAY
HUSBAND IS OLD	TABLE
KING	WEALTHY WOMAN
LAMP	WORD SPOKEN ON BEHALF

```
L A M P N M Y H E A D M Y H E A D F
S A D D L E D T H E A S S R O N L L
S N Y P S B E D E I D E H O S A O E
E T E S F E E T Z V Q X T P H M S S
R A L E T P R A Y E D M U E E O I H
T B E W Z A H S I L E E B N H W D B
S L M A E E F W B N Y N R E A Y N E
I E R C G R D F O Z O U I D D H A C
D A A K I N G S U N D H A E N T B A
R T C L E I E D E P G S H Y O L S M
E S T A H R F K L V O N C E S A U E
T O N P O J O N L I E N A S O E H W
T M U B S P R I N G H N C M N W K A
I E O M S E R V A N T C T H Y R O R
B F M D E V I E C N O C P I I L Q M
S O R O O F C H A M B E R U M L O T
C O M M A N D E R O F A R M Y E D H
W D V Y A W R O O D N I D O O T S W
```

Word Search 86

TEN COMMANDMENTS

Locate and loop only the words underlined in these commandments found in Exodus 20:3-17 (KJV).

"Thou shalt have no other gods before me."

"Thou shalt not make unto thee any graven image."

"Thou shalt not take the name of the Lord thy God in vain."

"Remember the sabbath day, to keep it holy."

"Honour thy father and thy mother."

"Thou shalt not kill."

"Thou shalt not commit adultery."

"Thou shalt not steal."

"Thou shalt not bear false witness against thy neighbor."

"Thou shalt not covet."

BONUS BIBLE TRIVIA

Nazareth to Bethlehem is approximately 70 miles as the crow flies. As the donkey trots, it's about a three day trip.

```
S  A  B  B  A  T  H  O  N  O  U  R
S  F  E  T  O  G  O  D  S  Q  E  O
E  A  A  P  E  T  A  K  E  M  S  B
N  T  R  T  H  V  W  I  E  R  L  H
T  H  R  E  H  T  O  M  N  O  A  G
I  E  R  O  F  E  B  C  R  S  F  I
W  R  M  A  K  E  N  D  L  H  T  E
S  V  H  Y  R  E  T  L  U  D  A  N
B  X  G  O  V  D  I  A  P  Y  I  A
S  T  E  A  L  K  L  E  F  A  Y  M
C  H  R  J  E  Y  E  Z  V  D  F  E
E  G  A  M  I  K  T  I  M  M  O  C
```

Word Search 87

TEN PLAGUES
(in the order they appear in Exodus 7-12)

BLOOD

FROGS

GNATS

FLIES

(plague) ON CATTLE

BOILS

HAIL

LOCUSTS

DARKNESS

DEATH

BONUS BIBLE TRIVIA

Herod was struck down by God, and his body
was eaten by worms. Acts 12:21-23

O	L	O	C	U	S	T	S
P	N	F	R	O	G	S	E
S	W	C	U	N	E	Q	I
B	X	T	A	N	R	B	L
L	U	T	K	T	V	O	F
O	S	R	A	E	T	I	Z
O	A	B	H	A	I	L	C
D	E	A	T	H	D	S	E

Word Search 88

TOWER OF BABEL

Why did the people in the land of Shinar want to build a tower with its top in the heavens? Find out in Genesis 11:1-9.

BABEL	LAND OF SHINAR
BEGINNING	MEN MIGRATED
BITUMEN	NOT UNDERSTAND
BRICKS	ONE LANGUAGE
BUILD	ONE PEOPLE
BURN	SCATTERED ABROAD
CITY	SETTLED
CONFUSE	SPEECH
FEW WORDS	THE LORD
FOUND A PLAIN	TOP IN THE HEAVENS
FROM THE EAST	TOWER

```
S C O T M E N M I G R A T E D
K N N F H D J S K C I R B A N
I G E N L E O D P E B M O H A
E T P V P Y L R X D A R S E T
G B E Q A I U O B C B A W C S
A E O F U E V W R A E R Z O R
U G P B H J H W D D L I G N E
G I L T S A E E H T M O R F D
N N E K O E R F H C Y R N U N
A N R U B E T M P T E Q L S U
L I S U T O W T I Y N E B E T
E N X T W C Z C L D T I P V O
N G A E B I T U M E N A P S N
O C R F N I A L P A D N U O F
S L A N D O F S H I N A R E T
```

Word Search 89

TO WHOM DOES GOD GIVE GRACE?

Locate and loop only the words underlined in this verse found in James 4:6 (KJV).

"But he <u>giveth</u> <u>more</u> <u>grace</u>. <u>Wherefore</u> he <u>saith</u>, God <u>resisteth</u> the <u>proud</u>, but giveth grace <u>unto</u> the <u>humble</u>."

BONUS BIBLE TRIVIA

God made the shadow on a sundial go back ten steps as a sign to Hezekiah. 2 Kings 20:11

R	E	S	I	S	T	E	T	H
Q	R	C	X	T	Z	V	T	U
U	O	Y	A	D	W	E	R	M
A	F	D	U	R	V	S	D	B
G	E	O	E	I	G	B	F	L
C	R	G	G	U	N	T	O	E
P	E	N	Q	H	U	K	R	S
L	H	T	I	A	S	O	I	O
R	W	J	P	W	M	V	T	M

Word Search 90

TRANSFIGURATION

Find out what happened when Jesus took Peter, James, and John up a high mountain in Matthew 17:1-8.

APPEARED	JOHN
BELOVED SON	JOHN THE BAPTIST
BRIGHT CLOUD	MOSES
DISCIPLES	PETER
ELIAS	RAIMENT WAS WHITE
FACE DID SHINE	SORE AFRAID
"HEAR YE HIM"	THREE TABERNACLES
HIGH MOUNTAIN	TRANSFIGURED
JAMES	UNDERSTOOD
JESUS	VOICE

BONUS BIBLE TRIVIA

The Gospel of Luke was written to Theophilus. Luke 1:3

```
R E T E P B E R C Y I U W S F S
V A P P E A R E D W Z S E E E O
B R I G H T C L O U D U L L N R
A E D M X V O I C E N T C P I E
D J L G E S K A M D H A P I H A
E L V O E N O S E O N R L C S F
R W S M V U T R M R S N E S D R
U P A Y T E S W E X Q E A I I A
G J E Z J T D B A N B G S D D I
I F N H O J A S H S L A E O E D
F C K O P T M U O D W I D Q C R
S X D X E S C S V N E H A U A D
N T H E A R Y E H I M B I W F Y
A M R Q F T N J U I S O J T R K
R H I G H M O U N T A I N G E P
T S I T P A B E H T N H O J H L
```

Word Search 91

TWELVE DISCIPLES

ANDREW

BARTHOLOMEW

JAMES (son of Alphaeus)

JAMES (son of Zebedee)

JOHN

JUDAS

MATTHEW

PETER

PHILIP

SIMON

THADDAEUS

THOMAS

BONUS BIBLE TRIVIA

When Nebuchadnezzar went insane, he grew
claws like a bird and hair like an eagle's
feathers, and ate grass like a cow. Daniel 4:33

```
B  Z  S  I  M  O  N  A  S  T  V
W  A  T  A  P  I  L  I  H  P  S
G  X  R  B  D  F  U  A  C  E  Y
D  T  J  T  H  U  D  E  M  T  I
N  H  T  K  H  D  J  A  P  E  M
U  O  O  S  A  O  J  Q  L  R  A
S  M  Y  E  V  M  L  D  A  R  T
Z  A  U  M  X  C  E  O  W  B  T
P  S  F  A  M  U  I  S  M  O  H
J  T  Q  J  O  H  N  K  G  E  E
N  V  H  R  L  A  N  D  R  E  W
```

Word Search 92

WEDDING AT CANA

Read all about Jesus' first miracle in John 2:1-11.

BRIDEGROOM

BRIM

CANA OF GALILEE

DISCIPLES

FIRKINS

GLORY

JESUS CALLED

MANIFESTED FORTH

MARRIAGE

MIRACLE

MOTHER OF JESUS

RULER OF THE FEAST

SERVANTS

SIX WATERPOTS

TASTED

WATER

WINE

BONUS BIBLE TRIVIA

Samson killed more people when he died than he did when he lived. Judges 16:30

```
R E T A W E T L A J W G Y C H
F U Y B M I R A C L E D B T U
D E L L A C S U S E J V R S Z
I K S E R V A N T S I O I I H
S I P B R U K F M X F R D X E
C V Q Z I O N G C D M Y E W S
I F A J A H F T E W I O G A D
P S I F G Y P T E A R V R T W
L B T R E J S Q H X B H O E C
E G Y U K E Z D I E K R O R D
S M E R F I K A N I F C M P E
F O J I O P N I H L N E G O T
D B N Q M L W S B N C S A T S
C A N A O F G A L I L E E S A
M O T H E R O F J E S U S R T
```

Word Search 93

WHAT IS FAITH?

Locate and loop only the words underlined in these verses found in Hebrews 11:1-3 (KJV).

"Now <u>faith</u> is the <u>substance</u> of <u>things</u> <u>hoped</u> for, the <u>evidence</u> of things <u>not seen</u>.

For by it the <u>elders</u> <u>obtained</u> a <u>good</u> <u>report</u>.

Through faith we <u>understand</u> that the <u>worlds</u> were <u>framed</u> by the <u>word of God</u>, so that things which are seen were not <u>made</u> of things which do <u>appear</u>."

BONUS BIBLE TRIVIA

Noah's ark had three stories. Genesis 6:16

S	W	E	V	I	D	E	N	C	E	R
R	T	O	R	A	E	P	P	A	D	V
E	H	B	R	Y	W	D	S	N	U	E
D	O	T	Z	D	O	X	A	S	F	C
L	P	A	I	O	O	T	B	D	R	N
E	E	I	G	A	S	F	C	L	A	A
A	D	N	E	R	F	D	G	R	M	T
H	N	E	E	S	T	O	N	O	E	S
M	A	D	E	L	N	F	I	W	D	B
G	N	T	R	O	P	E	R	O	J	U
U	M	Q	K	P	T	H	I	N	G	S

189

Word Search 94

WHAT IS LOVE?

Read all about it in 1 Corinthians 13.

(not) ARROGANT

BEARS (all things)

BELIEVES (all things)

(not) BOASTFUL

ENDURES (all things)

HOPES (all things)

(does not) INSIST (on its own way)

(not) IRRITABLE

(not) JEALOUS

KIND

NEVER (ends)

PATIENT

(does not) REJOICE (at wrong)

(not) RESENTFUL

(rejoices in the) RIGHT

(not) RUDE

I	A	R	R	O	G	A	N	T	R	A
B	R	S	E	R	U	D	N	E	P	C
J	B	R	D	E	R	F	S	H	A	G
H	E	I	I	I	J	E	E	O	T	K
L	A	A	M	T	N	N	V	P	I	E
O	R	P	L	T	A	S	E	E	E	C
Q	S	U	F	O	R	B	I	S	N	I
R	T	U	D	U	U	V	L	S	T	O
W	L	X	Y	E	Z	S	E	E	T	J
L	U	F	T	S	A	O	B	A	B	E
K	I	N	D	C	D	T	H	G	I	R

Word Search 95

WHAT SHALL WE DO TO INHERIT
ETERNAL LIFE?

Locate and loop only the words underlined in this verse found in Luke 10:27 (RSV).

"You shall love the Lord your God with all your heart, and with all your soul, and with all your strength, and with all your mind; and your neighbor as yourself."

BONUS BIBLE TRIVIA

The Holy Place in the Tabernacle contained three things—the lampstand, the wood table, and the consecrated bread. Hebrews 9:2

```
H   T   G   N   E   R   T   S
M   E   S   F   B   I   H   X
I   E   A   C   Y   A   J   T
N   V   U   R   L   O   R   D
D   O   Z   L   T   U   D   V
F   L   E   S   R   U   O   Y
H   A   W   G   O   D   E   S
N   E   I   G   H   B   O   R
```

Word Search 96

WHY DO WE SOMETIMES FAIL TO RECEIVE
WHEN WE ASK?

Locate and loop only the words underlined in this verse
found in James 4:3 (KJV).

"Ye ask, and receive not, because ye ask amiss, that ye
may consume it upon your lusts."

BONUS BIBLE TRIVIA

An ebenezer is a memorial stone. 1 Samuel 7:12

C	O	N	S	U	M	E	T
X	F	E	H	U	A	E	C
L	U	S	T	S	V	Y	V
Z	P	U	S	I	W	B	Y
Y	O	A	E	I	D	A	N
O	N	C	L	E	M	G	O
U	E	E	I	T	H	A	T
R	J	B	M	K	A	S	K

Word Search 97

WIDOW'S OIL

Find out how the widow was able to pay her debts in 2 Kings 4:1-7.

BORROW VESSELS

CREDITOR

CRIED TO ELISHA

FEAR THE LORD

HOUSE

HUSBAND IS DEAD

JAR OF OIL

MAIDSERVANT

PAY DEBTS

POUR

SELL

SHUT THE DOOR

SLAVES

STOPPED FLOWING

TWO CHILDREN

WIFE

BONUS BIBLE TRIVIA

Seraphim (the plural of seraph) are the angel-type beings Isaiah saw. Isaiah 6

```
G  V  T  N  A  V  R  E  S  D  I  A  M  H
E  N  I  W  C  Z  H  W  R  G  D  B  A  U
A  D  I  H  O  U  S  E  U  R  F  H  X  S
R  P  L  W  Y  C  S  U  O  J  S  M  T  B
O  T  I  N  O  K  H  L  P  I  Q  B  V  A
T  X  O  S  W  L  E  I  L  O  E  R  L  N
I  E  F  Y  L  H  F  E  L  D  A  W  C  D
D  B  O  D  T  A  O  D  Y  D  F  I  Z  I
E  K  R  R  P  T  V  A  E  S  R  F  O  S
R  T  A  Y  D  V  P  E  R  P  X  E  L  D
C  E  J  E  Q  M  Z  W  S  N  P  U  N  E
F  E  I  G  A  S  E  L  L  F  D  O  B  A
C  R  O  O  D  E  H  T  T  U  H  S  T  D
C  B  O  R  R  O  W  V  E  S  S  E  L  S
```

Word Search 98

WOMAN AT THE WELL

Find out what Jesus said to the woman at Jacob's well in John 4:1-26.

DEPARTED	MESSIAH
DRAW WATER	NEVER THIRST AGAIN
DRINK	NO DEALINGS
ETERNAL LIFE	PASS THROUGH
FIVE HUSBANDS	SAMARIA
GALILEE	SIXTH HOUR
JACOB'S WELL	SYCHAR
JESUS	TESTIMONY
JEW	WEARY
LEFT JUDEA	WENT AWAY TO CITY
LEFT WATER JAR	WOMAN
LIVING WATER	

```
W R U C I K Y E A G W E A R Y N
L E F T W A T E R J A R V J I O
I T N E H G U O R H T S S A P D
V A Z T D J D F D A W B G C H E
I W I E A R L X E I O A A O S A
N W T R I W P V P S T M L B R L
G A W N A Q A N A S U X I S Y I
W R K A V M S Y R E Z B L W D N
A D W L Y C A I T M A T E E X G
T Q E L U K H S E O S H E L N S
E L R I W T U F D S C U I L O V
R M G F R U O H H T X I S J P T
F I V E H U S B A N D S T E T J
X D V U A T E S T I M O N Y J E
L E F T J U D E A Y E V I B G W
N A M O W F W C H Z S Y C H A R
```

Word Search 99

WOMEN OF THE BIBLE

ABIGAIL	LEAH
AHINOAM	MARTHA
BATHSHEBA	MARY
BILHAH	MARY MAGDALENE
DAMARIS	MIRIAM
DEBORAH	NAOMI
DELILAH	QUEEN OF SHEBA
DINAH	QUEEN VASHTI
DORCAS	RACHEL
ELIZABETH	RAHAB
ESTHER	REBEKAH
EVE	RUTH
HAGAR	SALOME
HANNAH	SARAH
JEZEBEL	ZILPAH
JUDITH	ZIPPORAH

```
M A O N I H A E J E Z E B E L
D A M A R I S S A C R O D V E
E S R A G A H T J X D I N A H
B A Z Y B A T H S H E B A L C
O R V R M T P E B L N B B D A
R A E O A A D R I S I Q E U R
A H V J R F G Z W G Y L H E A
H T E U Y C A D A H I A S H N
A R B D I B D I A L P Z F A R
R A G I E I L T A L E L O N E
O M V T X L E H I M E M N N B
P R H H P H C Z O A I N E A E
P M I R I A M L H O A U E H K
I Q S R A H A B M Y H T U R A
Z K I T H S A V N E E U Q W H
```

Word Search 100

ZACCHAEUS

Find out why Zacchaeus climbed the sycamore tree in Luke 19:1-10.

CROWD	RICH
GIVE TO THE POOR	SALVATION
GUEST	SINNER
HALF OF GOODS	SMALL OF STATURE
HOUSE	SYCAMORE TREE
JERICHO	TAX COLLECTOR
JESUS	ZACCHAEUS
RESTORE FOURFOLD	

BONUS BIBLE TRIVIA

Jacob made the coat that he gave to Joseph, his favorite son. Genesis 37:3

```
Z N F Z A C C H A E U S L R D
H S D O O G F O F L A H P L B
G T M D B F J H X L V J O D Z
I N V A Z D L J V T X F H B S
V Q Y R L A S A U W R F P I Y
E M D E I L T C H U G O N K C
T E W J U I O G O S Y N B Q A
O C O W O A H F U X E D F Z M
T H R N P T E I S R N J R V O
H F C L D R B H E T S E U G R
E C R I O G X I T U A V E Z E
P W O T R S K Y S U Q T A I T
O A S E Y E C E O M K Q U W R
O E G M S U J C E I H C I R E
R O T C E L L O C X A T G A E
```

Word Search 101

ROYAL WOMEN OF THE BIBLE

ABI	JEDIDAH
ABISHAG	JEHOADDAN
ASENATH	JEHOSHEBA
ATHALIAH	JERUSHA
BATHSHEBA	MAACHAH
CANDACE	MERAB
COZBI	MICHAL
ESTHER	NEHUSHTA
HADASSAH	RIZPAH
HAGGITH	TAHPENES
HAMUTAL	VASHTI
HEPHZIBAH	ZEBUDAH
HERODIAS	ZIBIAH
JECHOLIAH	

```
M I C H A L H T H T A N E S A
C O Z B I A A E G A H S I B A
B R I C H H P S A I D O R E H
G R T C P H J N E H U S H T A
N O A E Z J E C H O L I A H X
O A N I A T H A L I A H Y I E
M E B E H A I B I Z E E B S J
S A A B E H S O H E J A T L E
H M E R A B A Z R A Y H Z A C
Z E B U D A H D R I E I A T A
E D V A S H T I I R Z Y O U D
A B E H S H T A B D O P N M N
J E H O A D D A N J E S A A A
W J D K J E R U S H A J S H C
Y H A S S A D A H T I G G A H
```

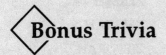

Bonus Trivia

Solomon had 700 wives and 300 concubines.
Anniversaries must have been a problem.

Word Search 102

MORE WOMEN IN THE BIBLE

AHOLAH	MAIA
AHOLIBAH	MARTHA
ANNA	MIRIAM
APPHIA	NAOMI
BITHIAH	ORPAH
CHLOE	PHOEBE
CLAUDIA	PUAH
DELILAH	SALOME
DORCAS	SAPPHIRA
EUDIA	SHELOMITH
HANNAH	SHIPRAH
HULDAH	SYNTYCHE
JAEL	ZERESH
JOANNA	ZERUIAH
JOCHEBED	ZIPPORAH
MAACAH	

```
A N N A E E D C E B E O H P M
D R I A P H E O L H C F K I W
K P E I R H C E R S Y C M Q D
D E U D I A A Y M C W O S A G
E S H U S J H I T A A W A I J
L M A A M H J H U N R S P H O
I H K L D A A O M R Y T P P A
L A J C O L I U C I E S H P N
A B W K O M U A P H R Z I A N
H I O H T F E H V Y E I R Y A
A L A H A R O P P I Z B A K A
P O Z F B B I T H I A H E M Z
R H A N N A H H A C A A M D G
O A G P T B H T I M O L E H S
H A R J H A R P I H S E R E Z
```

Bonus Trivia

The name Abraham (Abram) is mentioned
in the Bible 188 times. Sarah is mentioned
only 31 times.

Word Search 103

CAPTAINS & COMMANDERS IN THE BIBLE

ABIEZER

ABNER

ARIOCH

ASAHEL

BENAIAH

BIDKAR

DODAI

GOD

HANANIAH

HELDAI

HELEZ

IRA

JEHOHANAN

JEPHTHAH

JOAB

MAHARAI

NAAMAN

NEBUZARADAN

OMRI

PEKAH

PELATIAH

PEREZ

PHICOL

RABSARIS

SHOPHACK

SIBBECAI

SISERA

TARTAN

ZEBADIAH

ZIMRI

```
H U H W G H A I D A B E Z H Y
A Z I R A K D I B O N K F A P
I E B A S A V I A L A T H H J
T L E A R I R M O S M N E T E
A E N B P A S I C Q A D L H H
L H A I F S H E O T A M D P O
E C I E R A O A R C N G A E H
P Z A Z G H F A M A H I I J A
J C H E O E T M Z I M R I T N
O T J R D L H A I N A N A H A
A A B N E R A B S A R I S D N
B I A D O D N Z E R E P A J I
N E B U Z A R A D A N G M U F
B P H I C O L S H O P H A C K
M P E K A H S I B B E C A I U
```

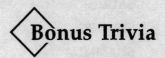
Adam was 130 years old when Seth was born. Genesis 5:3

Word Search 104

SPIED & LIED

ABRAHAM	JUDAH
AMMIEL	LEVI
ASHER	NAHBI
BARJESUS	OSHEA
CAIN	PALTI
DAN	PASHUR
GAD	PHAROAH
GADDI	RACHEL
GADDIEL	REBEKAH
GEHAZI	REUBEN
GEUEL	SAPPHIRA
HEROD	SATAN
IGAL	SAUL
ISAAC	SETHUR
ISSACHAR	SHAMMUA
JACOB	SIMEON
JEHU	ZEBULUN
JONATHAN	

```
U D I S A A C N Y S S R L A N
S H A M M U A Z E T A A B S Q
U H E J D H L T N H I R U S N
K P P S B C H E C O A V A L A
R H A I U U A A H H E T E E H
E A L M R S S I A C A M G L T
B O T B M S E M N N A A I I A
E R I D I I Q J S P R R Z S N
K A N E B U E R R I D A C L O
A H B L P H J L H A H B X E J
H P A N E U E P G E B M A I G
K G A R D U P Q G J O X S D A
I D O A E A E H S O C A H D D
R D H G S O R U H S A P E A D
S Z E B U L U N I S J L R G I
```

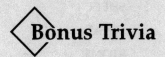

Bonus Trivia

Bethlehem means "house of bread."

Word Search 105

FIVE LETTER WORDS

BEGAT	HORSE
BLOOD	IMMER
BOZEZ	INDIA
BURNT	INNER
CHIOS	JESUS
CHIUN	JOGLI
CHODE	LIVER
CHURL	MANNA
CLIFF	NEVER
CURSE	OFFER
DAVID	SACAR
DEATH	SENEH
DWELL	SEVEN
FAITH	SHEEP
FAVOR	SOTAI
FIRST	STONE
FLEET	STUDY
FLESH	TEACH
HOMER	UMMAH
HONEY	VOICE

```
C H O R S E V R H T A E D Z M
H H O H N H A O I F F I L C T
I R D O O C C A I N D I A P C
O H T A A N T A F C R E M M I
S S O S V O E L E A E U K V S
F I F M S I I Y V T V D O E E
L Y L H E V D V M X E O V K D
N L E G E R F Z X A N E R U O
I E E R O N L X Y S N P P A H
P G T W O J E X F U R N C R C
B L O O D I S S I E Z L A M T
F A I T H N H H F E R V W Y N
J E S U S N C F Z U M M A H R
U C U R S E O O H T A G E B U
S T U D Y R B C J F I R S T B
```

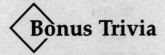

Bonus Trivia

Eliud was Jesus' great-great-great-grand-father. Matthew 1:15

213

Word Search 106

MORE FIVE LETTER WORDS

ALARM	KNOCK
ALOES	LIGHT
ALOOF	MOSES
ALPHA	NIGHT
BARNS	OMEGA
BASER	PRIVY
BLIND	RABBI
BRIDE	RIGHT
CANST	ROYAL
CHILD	SNAKE
DRAVE	SPEAK
DREAM	STANK
ENTER	STARE
FEAST	STEAD
FINER	TRUTH
GRAVE	VILER
HONOR	VIPER
IDLES	VISIT
IGEAL	WAXEN
JAPHO	WOMAN
JUDGE	WORLD
KEDAR	

```
A S Y R G F S T V M R A D E K
L A B E R O N S K I R E T N E
O P G S A O R A T R L A J E K
E R C A V L A E K E A E L X I
S I A B E A B F B W A B R A G
P V N K G V R O N O H D B W E
E Y S A D Y A U T R U T H I A
A M T L U J B R I D E D P T L
K O T P J K T L D Y L A Y O R
R S Z H N H C O I R T H G I R
E E F A G D P O O N O M E G A
P S T I C I R W N U D L I H C
I S N A N I L E K K W O M A N
V I S I T E E R A T S E L D I
K J A P H O R C A M E K A N S
```

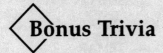

Bonus Trivia

Noah was a healthy 600 years old when God
sent the flood. Genesis 7:6

Word Search 107

ABRAHAM'S PROGENY

ABDEEL	KEDEMAH
AMALEK	KENAZ
ASHER	KORAH
BENJAMIN	LEVI
DAN	MASSA
DINAH	MIBSAM
DUMAH	MISHMA
ELIPHAZ	NAPHISH
GAD	NAPHTALI
GATAM	OMAR
HADAD	REUBEN
ISSACHAR	REUEL
JALAM	SIMEON
JETUR	TEMA
JEUSH	TEMAR
JOSEPH	ZEBULUN
JUDAH	ZEPHO

```
U D E J O S E P H I J E U S H
H H A D U J R D S N R U T E J
A S G N H A A S P E T I U F R
D R J A M G A S S A M E W H E
A V M E T C T I B A N G M S U
D U T G H A M H M M U L G A B
D D D A K E M A D H L Y B E E
D I R N O E S S H S U F E L N
Q N O N A B D H P I B K N I A
Z A L H I P L E S M E E J P P
A H E M P E H R M I Z L A H H
N Y E O V E Y I A A T A M A T
E O D I M E Z Y S F H M I Z A
K E B S J A L A M H H A N F L
Q K A V K O R A H R E U E L I
```

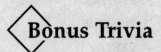

Bonus Trivia

A cubit is eighteen inches long. That means the ark was 5400 inches long and 900 inches wide. Genesis 6:15

Word Search 108

SIX LETTER WORDS

ACCEPT	LIFTED
ALBEIT	MEMBER
BARBED	MIGRON
BARKOS	ORACLE
BASKET	PERISH
BETTER	QUIVER
BOWMEN	RACHEL
CANKER	RAISED
DESERT	SARAPH
ENTIRE	SAVING
EXCEPT	SPIRIT
FINISH	SPOKEN
FRIEND	SYCHAR
HEAVEN	TONGUE
HINDER	VESTRY
JEWISH	

```
R E T T E B T R E S E D C P H
B M R J G F R I E N D Q T L J
O M B W N C A N K E R Y R G E
W T I R I P S X B T I E B L A
M H E A V E N R U J E W I S H
E H H P A R A S P E R I S H U
N L S T S B P A L I F T E D E
S S C I O W S Y C H A R I E P
N O W A N N L E H C A R T E R
O K E R R I G D N V E E Q X E
R R R E E O F U E E K P S C V
G A I B D U G C E S K M T E I
I B T M N J H K A T I O U P U
M F N E I Q X B E R E A P T Q
D U E M H I I P O Y Z L R S M
```

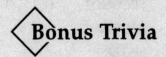

Bonus Trivia

Noah died at 950 years of age. Genesis 6:14

Word Search 109

MORE SIX LETTER WORDS

BURNED	MUSICK
CHRIST	NARROW
CORBAN	NATION
FATHER	NATURE
HITHER	NIMROD
HOLDEN	NINETY
HUNTER	OFFEND
HUSHAI	ORATOR
IMPUTE	OWNERS
INTENT	PRAISE
JEARIM	PROFIT
KETTLE	REAPER
LUHITH	SECOND
MEHIDA	SEORIM
MELCHI	SISTER
MELODY	SPRING
MOTHER	

```
I E T U P M I L S R E N W O R
S E C O N D S U R E T S I S M
Q T I F O R P E M E L O D Y T
M R G I K D R F O M U S I C K
N E R N E N E C O R B A N K R
A H E T T E T D L N I N E T Y
T T H E T F N F E C L M X D J
I I T N L F U A N N N T O J H
O H A T E O H S T N R R L I U
N U F E S I A R P U M U R H S
E L W O R R A N B I R T B C H
D R E A P E R C N U H E U L A
L C H R I S T R O T A R O E I
O V J E A R I M R E H T O M F
H G S P R I N G M E H I D A X
```

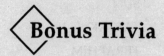

Bonus Trivia

Jacob and Rachel were cousins. Genesis 29:10

Word Search 110

IDOLS & FALSE GODS IN THE BIBLE

ADRAM	GOLDEN CALF
ANAM	HERMES
ASHERAH	MOON
ASHIMA	NEHUSHTAN
ASHTORETH	NERGAL
BAAL	NIBHAZ
BAALZEBUB	NISROCH
BEAST	PLANETS
BELLY	POLLUX
CASTOR	RIMMON
CHEMOSH	SILVER
CHIUN	STARS
DAGON	SUN
DEMONS	TARTAK
DIANA	TERAPHIM
DRAGON	ZEUS
GOLD	

```
S Q D I A N A V H A B N K N F
I Z S N M G H P S A E H O P G
L X T E A N O H A H R G R O I
V Z E R R M I L U R A E O Y M
E A N G D M Z S D D O R H L Z
R H A A A E H P R E B T N S D
X B L L B T N N A O N E S U A
U I P U A H C S U T C C L A S
L N B N E H H M E I A H A L C
L D O R E T N R D N H R H L Y
O N M M O S A O O E E C T L F
P E O R A P R M G Z M T P A R
S S E N H T M A C A E O D A K
H T A I F I X G T Z R U N B G
H M M Z R X B E A S T D S S V
```

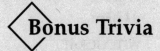

Bonus Trivia

In the entire book of Esther, God is not mentioned once.

Word Search 111

SINS & SINNERS IN THE BIBLE

ADULTERY	MISCHIEF
CHEAT	MURDER
CRUELTY	PERJURY
DECEIT	PERVERSE
DRUNKARD	PRIDE
ENVY	PROFANE
EXTORTION	REBELLION
HATRED	SLANDER
HYPOCRISY	SLUGGARD
IDOLATRY	STRIFE
INIQUITY	STUBBORN
LAZY	TEMPER
LIES	THIEF
LUST	VANITY
MALICE	WITCHCRAFT

G	U	Q	N	O	I	T	R	O	T	X	E	P	P	H
E	G	S	M	S	I	N	I	Q	U	I	T	Y	E	Y
T	L	T	I	T	S	L	A	N	D	E	R	C	R	P
F	A	U	S	R	N	I	D	Y	U	R	M	F	V	O
A	Z	B	C	I	U	E	T	R	F	E	U	C	E	C
R	Y	B	H	F	B	S	P	E	O	P	R	R	R	R
C	X	O	I	E	U	E	I	T	D	M	D	U	S	I
H	B	R	E	L	R	H	H	L	M	E	E	E	E	S
C	V	N	F	J	T	P	M	U	S	T	R	L	B	Y
T	H	A	U	O	R	A	I	D	O	L	A	T	R	Y
I	I	R	N	O	L	B	T	A	E	H	C	Y	A	P
W	Y	E	F	I	R	E	B	E	L	L	I	O	N	H
K	R	A	C	U	T	I	D	R	U	N	K	A	R	D
P	N	E	Z	E	F	Y	D	R	A	G	G	U	L	S
E	N	V	Y	Z	D	E	D	I	R	P	C	Q	G	G

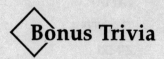

Bonus Trivia

An omer is equivalent to 2 quarts.

Word Search 112

SINNERS & VICTIMS

ABSALOM	HOPHNI
AMNON	JEZEBEL
BALAAM	LOT
BALAK	MOAB
BATHSHEBA	ONAN
BILHAH	PERGAMOS
CORINTH	PHINEAS
COZBI	RAHAB
DAVID	REUBEN
DINAH	SAMSON
GIBEAH	SHECHEM
GOMER	SODOM
GOMORRAH	TAMAR
HEROD	THYATIRA
HERODIAS	ZIMRI

```
J H S H X O B A L A A M N O N
P X O L C L Z J M O L A S B A
E W D A O O N E B U E R Z E G
R Z O T V L R B K A L A B D U
G O M E R S A I D O R E H B G
A R H O P H N I N N J P I I L
M D N O S M A S Y T Y L B Y J
O A B E H S H T A B H E H O E
S Z J O R K T D O A A A B M Z
E U W O N A B I H H N S A E E
I R M I Z A M V Y I F I H H B
H E R O D D N A D B C B A C E
P H I N E A S D T Y A Z R E L
T W H A R R O M O G A O W H A
V P T H Y A T I R A K C M S L
```

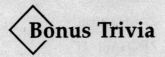

Bonus Trivia

David's warriors could shoot arrows right and left handed. 1 Chronicles 12:2

Word Search 113

DREAMERS & VISIONARIES IN THE BIBLE

ABIMELECH	JOSEPH
ABRAHAM	LABAN
ANANIAS	MAGI
BAALAM	MARY
BAKER	MIDIANITE
CUPBEARER	NAHUM
DANIEL	NEBUCHADNEZZAR
EZEKIEL	PAUL
IDDO	PETER
ISAIAH	PHAROAH
JACOB	SALOME
JAMES	SAMUEL
JEREMIAH	SOLOMON
JOB	ZACHARIUS
JOHN	ZECHARIAH

```
P H A R O A H N O M O L O S I
J A H H C U P B E A R E R I N
O I C A N A N I A S B U A W A
B M E E L E I K E Z E M H C B
A E L B T V R C M U H A N J A
A R E Y A I H E S P H S R S L
B E M R L A N A L X E Q U E B
R J I A Q O L A I J G T I J O
A U B M D O H A I R O N E C C
H U A D M X Y E M D A H B R A
A B I E S E M A J D I H N U J
M U Z A C H A R I U S M C A M
Y I G A M N Z H P E S O J E T
N E B U C H A D N E Z Z A R Z
L U A P B A K E R I S A I A H
```

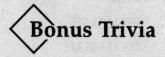

Bonus Trivia

Manna tasted like honey wafers. Exodus 16:31

Word Search 114

PROPHETS IN THE BIBLE

AARON	JESUS
AGABUS	JOEL
AHIJAH	JOHN
AMOS	JONAH
ANNA	MALACHI
AZARIAH	MICAH
BARSABBUS	MICAIAH
CAIAPHAS	MIRIAM
DANIEL	MOSES
DEBORAH	NAHUM
ELIJAH	NATHAN
GAD	SAMUEL
HABAKKUK	SAUL
HOSEA	SHEMAIAH
HULDAH	ZECHARIAH
ISAIAH	ZEDEKIAH
JEREMIAH	ZEPHANIAH

```
H H S S I H G N H A R O B E D
A W U V A S A H A I A C I M W
J M B L V M A J Q H A R N G H
I I B N D I U I I G U A O A I
H C A H M A N E A L T M I N B
A A S E A H H B L H E R D B H
C H R Y O N U C A I A P H A S
K E A J L S O N Y H B S I Z A
J U B I L E O J C J H R E A M
M H K M N M I E S E A D M A T
A M Y K M A Z N M Z E O L J A
I O L U A S H A A K S A F E A
R S K G E B I P I D C Z S S N
I E D E A A A A E H F O Y U N
M S C M H D H H I Z H I T S A
```

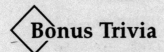

Bonus Trivia

In ancient Israel, men closed a deal by
exchanging sandals. Ruth 4:7

Word Search 115

FIREPOWER & VICTIMS

ACHAN	JERUSALEM
AI	JOAB
BEAST	JOSHUA
BENHADAD	JUDAH
BENJAMIN	MAGOG
BOZRAH	MOAB
EGYPT	NEBUCHADNEZZAR
ELIJAH	PHAROAH
EPHESIANS	PHILISTINES
GAZA	RABBAH
GEZER	SAMSON
GOD	SODOM
GOMORRAH	SOLDIERS
HAZAEL	TEMAN
HAZOR	TYRE
ISRAEL	ZIMRI
JERICHO	

```
J I H A J I L E A R T S A E B
E S G G B A O M C A H M S N K
R G O I A N Y B H Z A O R I H
I N D Q P Z A M A Z B D E M A
C E O X N O A E N E B O I A R
H Z S S J E B L D N A S D J R
O J I A M O R A J D R N L N O
H U J M Z A D S O A R A O E M
A D N R R A S U S H O I S B O
Z A A R H I O R H C Z S R G G
A H M N T Y R E U U A E E O W
E L E A R S I J A B H H Z G V
L B T P Y G E G A E S P E A I
J Y H A O R A H P N T E G M P
D J S E N I T S I L I H P J A
```

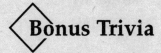

Bonus Trivia

The Levites had a mandatory requirement age of 50 years. Numbers 8:25

Word Search 116

PRISONERS, EXILES, & CAPTIVES

AZARIAH	JESHUA
BIGVAI	JESUS
BILSHAN	JOHN
CAIN	JOSEPH
DANIEL	LOT
ESTHER	MANASSEH
HAGAR	MARY
ISAIAH	MISPERETH
ISHMAEL	MORDECAI
ITTAI	NOAH
JACOB	PAUL
JEHOAZ	PETER
JEPHTHAH	RAAMIAH
JEREMIAH	ZEDEKIAH

```
I C Z E D E K I A H N E J I D
H T A O G Q L V X O R E S A J
R P T I V Q F D A E S A N M E
A E E A N I W H T H I I R O R
Z Y H S I U D E U A E M N R E
A M R T O G P A H L Q C A D M
R L U M S J K M H S B O H E I
I D N L I E J A A I L U S C A
A T O J J S H E J R O F L A H
H T O A R T P I H E Y N I I Z
O H C A H Q A E A O S L B L V
N O G P Z C H T R V A U U R F
B A E H K B P B R E G Z S A O
H J Q D I M Q W L M T I M H P
I O I H E S S A N A M H B Q X
```

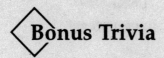

Bonus Trivia

Ham, Noah's son, built Ninevah. Genesis 10:11

Word Search 117

MORE PRISONERS, EXILES, & CAPTIVES

ABIGAIL	JEHOIACHIN
ABIJAH	JEROBOAM
AGAG	JUNIAS
AHINOAM	MALLUCH
AMOK	MICAIAH
ARISTARCHUS	NAHAMANI
BAANAH	NEHEMIAH
BARABBAS	NEHUM
BILGAH	SALLU
BINNUI	SAMSON
EZRA	SILAS
HANANI	STEPHEN
HATTUSH	UNNI
HOSHEA	ZERUBBABEL
IDDO	

```
H A N A N I H C A I O H E J N
O D O N A M A O B O R E J J O
S L Z E H D N I U N N I B U S
H J E H I Z E B I L G A H N M
E G L P N K H P E V B L R I A
A I E E O B U Q H Z P R S A S
U N B T A K M L Q P R E Y S O
L A A S M N E H E M I A H A D
L M B R H C U L L A M H Z B D
A A B M I C A I A H D E H B I
S H U L K O M A G A G A A A N
Y A R I S T A R C H U S J R N
O N E V V H S U T T A H I A U
X L Z H A N A A B R U E B B Y
S A L I S G L I A G I B A N J
```

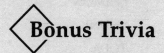
Paul was a tentmaker. Acts 18:1-3

Word Search 118

JACOB'S PROGENY

ARELI	JAHLEEL
ARODI	JAMIN
ASHBEL	JEMUEL
BECHER	JOB
BELA	KOHATH
BERIAH	MALCHIEL
ELON	MERARI
ERI	OHAD
EZBON	PUVAH
GERSHON	SERAH
HAGGI	SERED
HAMUL	SHAUL
HEBER	SHIMON
HEZRON	SHUNI
IMNAH	TOLA
ISHVAH	ZIPHION
ISHVI	ZOHAR
JACHIN	

```
N T O H A D M D J A H L E E L
L O Y N T E N L R E A R E L I
U L T W R O E O B S H I M O N
A A P A I I D E D N I H C A J
H H R H H I R E A I N U H S G
S I P C S B R H B E R I A H T
Z I L H I E C I T E Q W W S O
Z A V B S C K M G A L Q W E O
M A L O A H J N H E H A L R E
H V V J Q E J A W L R O U A Z
P E K N M R H H E T N S K H B
U C R U I A A B X W P D H P O
V H E I G M H H L U M A H O N
A L S G F S A E O H E Z R O N
H M I K A B V J X Z I V H S I
```

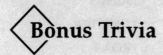

Bonus Trivia

Luke was a medical doctor. Colossions 4:14

Word Search 119

NEW TESTAMENT CHURCHES

ACHAIA

ANTIOCH

AZOTUS

BEREA

CAESAREA

CENCHREA

CILICIA

CORINTH

CRETE

CYRENE

DAMASCUS

DERBE

GALILEE

JOPPA

LAODICEA

LIBYA

LYDDA

LYSTRA

PERGA

PERGAMUM

PHOENICIA

PONTUS

PTOLEMAIS

ROME

SALAMIS

SAMARIA

SIDON

SYRIA

TARSUS

THYATIRA

TROAS

TYRE

```
S J A R C I L I C I A L T H S
I C O I O Z H H L S S Y Y M U
D M R P R M M M A E U S R A C
O D B E P Y E C O T S T E L S
N P E X T A S O D H R R O A A
L Z R T O E A R I Y A A L Z M
E C E P L R I I C A T A X M A
C Y A E E H A N E T M A I I D
E R H R M C H T A I E C C A S
E E C G A N C H S R G I Y S A
L N O A I E A D A A N B A G M
I E I M S C E S D E I O R V A
L F T U T R E D O L R E T H R
A L N M B A Y H F T P W R T I
G I A E C L P S U T N O P J A
```

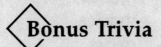 Bonus Trivia

Did you know that when Jesus died, saints rose from the dead and walked around Jerusalem? Matthew 27:52-53

Word Search 120

PAUL'S MISSIONARY JOURNEYS

AMPHIPOLIS	MITYLENE
ANTIOCH	MYRA
APPOLONIA	MYSIA
ASIA	NEAPOLIS
ATHENS	PATARA
ATTALIA	PERGA
BEREA	RHODES
CAPPADOCIA	SALAMIS
CENCHREA	SAMOS
COLOSSE	SELEUCIA
COS	SMYRNA
CYPRUS	SYRIA
GALATIA	TARSUS
ICONIUM	THRACE
LYCIA	TROAS
LYSTRA	TYRE
MACEDONIA	

```
C E N C H R E A M C S A M O S
P T R O A S A U A S U R P Y C
A E R E B T F P I A G R E P O
T Y R E T L P L R H O D E S H
A G D A A A O S E L E U C I A
R C L I D P M A C E D O N I A
A I S O I S N M I T Y L E N E
A Y C H N T Q E S S O L O C Z
M I P E I A I N O L O P P A A
A M H O U A S H M U I N O C I
A T C N B J S I L O P A E N T
A H S Y R I A Y A L Y M N A A
E C A R H T C O S L Y C I A L
S I M A L A S T A R S U S J A
V S M Y R N A V A R T S Y L G
```

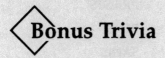

Bonus Trivia

Animals have to answer to God, too.
Genesis 9:5

Word Search 121

WEEPERS IN THE BIBLE

ABRAHAM	JOB
BENJAMIN	JOHN
BILDAD	JOSIAH
CONGREGATION	LEVITES
DAVID	MARY
ELIPHAZ	MERCHANTS
ELISHA	MOSES
ESAU	NEHEMIAH
ESTHER	ORPAH
EZRA	PAUL
HAGAR	PETER
HEZEKIAH	PHALTIEL
ISHMAEL	PRIESTS
ISRAEL	RUTH
JACOB	SAUL
JEREMIAH	TOPHAR
JESUS	WIDOWS

```
A I M P B E N J A M I N L P M
J R N O I T A G E R G N O C A
O B Z B S T S E I R P P J C H
S O H E O P A U L K H E O N A
I J A R M M O S E S P T H E R
A T P A G Z S E A E H E N H B
H E R H L A T T M S A R E E A
H Y O P E H N I H A L S E M Z
A D D O A P A V S U T L H I S
I B A T R I H E I H I S T A J
K O D V S L C L E S E A U H E
E C L Z I E R R H U L L R V S
Z A I A V D E A W I D O W S U
E J B F A G M O U N T A I N S
H S H A G A R J E R E M I A H
```

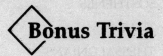

Bonus Trivia

Paul was beaten five times and shipwrecked
three. 2 Corinthians 11:24-25

Word Search 122

LETTER WRITERS & RECIPIENTS

ARTAXERXES	JOAB
COLOSSIANS	JOHN
DARIUS	JUDE
DAVID	LYSIAS
ELDER	MANASSEH
ELIJAH	NOBLES
EPHESIANS	PAUL
EPHRAIM	PETER
FELIX	PHILEMON
GAIUS	PHILIPPIANS
GALATIANS	ROMANS
JAMES	SENNACHERIB
JEHORAM	SOSTHENES
JEHU	TITUS
JEWS	THESSALONIANS
JEZEBEL	TOBIAH

```
L Y S I A S G A L A T I A N S
S S N A I N O L A S S E H T T
U T A C L E B E Z E J J Y O E
I J I E O J O P X L A C B H B
R E P T L L E J H M U I E A I
A S P R U D O W E I A A I J R
D E I H F S E S S H L G P I E
J X L E R M D R S N O E W L H
O R I V D A A G B I A R M E C
H E H X V U I N A A A M A O A
N X P I X B J M A I O N O M N
J A D X I L E F D S U J S R N
E T U C R N O B L E S S H S E
H R E T E P S O S T H E N E S
U A W E P H E S I A N S H P C
```

The term "scapegoat" comes from the use of a goat that was to receive the sins of the people and be released into the wilderness. Leviticus 16:10

Word Search 123

CURSERS & CURSEES # 1

ACHAN	JOTHAM
ARABIA	LORD
BALAAM	MEDESELAM
BITTER WATER	MEN
BOZRAH	MEROZ
BUZ	PETER
CAIN	PRIESTS
CANAAN	REBEKAH
CHRIST	REMNANT
FIG TREE	SERPENT
GOD	SHESHACH
GROUND	SHILOH
ISRAEL	TEMA
JEHOIAKIM	UZ
JESUS	WOMAN
JEWS	ZIMRI

```
X H N B I T T E R W A T E R T
B A A G O D Z B L L C S S U E
M K M D N O X U O H E H K W E
A E O S R U B E R Z E A I P R
L B W E T A J I D S R R R N T
E E M M L S S N H A M A E S G
S R N A I T E A I I M M H S I
E Y A Q C K C I Z A P E Y H F
D M H T T H A D R G C O T I U
E A C N N G N I N P E J P L O
M I A E A L A G O U E Z U O S
Q B X P N U A C X H O T G H W
C A Z R M V N P Q C E R E K E
B R U E E J O T H A M J G R J
W A H S R Z U B S U S E J A M
```

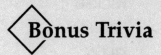

Bonus Trivia

Moses was four years old when Pharaoh's
daughter found him in the basket. Acts 7:20-21

Word Search 124

CURSERS & CURSEES # 2

ABIMELECH

AMMON

ASHDOD

ASHKELON

AZZAH

DAVID

DEDAN

EARTH

EDOM

EGYPT

EKRON

EVIL

GENERATION

IDUMEA

ISLES

JACOB

JEREMIAH

JERUSALEM

JUDAH

KING

MOAB

PHAROAH

PHILISTINES

SERVANT

SHECHEM

SHIMEI

TYRUS

WICKED

ZEDEKIAH

ZIDON

```
F R I S L E S I T N A V R E S
D I V A D N O L E K H S A F J
E Z M H A D U J W I C K E D J
D D A A E M U D I M I Z K D A
A T O V P H A R O A H N H N C
N I E M H M U S F S J Y C O O
T E A Q I E Z L D H E L E I B
Y M R P L L H A Z D R G L T Y
R I T P I A A M S O E Q E A Z
U H H E S S I M H D M Z M R L
S S A G T U K O E L I I I E G
M K Z Y I R E N C I A D B N Q
O I Z P N E D R H V H O A E K
A N A T E J E L E E P N S G M
B G H O S D Z F M R N O R K E
```

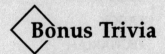

Bonus Trivia

Nahor, Abraham's grandfather's name, means "snorer."

Word Search 125

PRIESTS OF THE BIBLE

AARON	HOPHNI
ABIHU	IMMER
ABISHUA	ITHAMAR
AHIAH	JEHOIADA
AHIMELECH	JOSHUA
AHITUB	MAASEIAH
AMARIAH	MATTAN
AMAZIAH	NADAB
ANANIAS	PHINEHAS
ANNAS	POTIPHERA
AZARIAH	SERAIAH
ELEAZAR	URIAH
ELI	URIJAH
ELIASHIB	ZADOK
EZRA	ZECHARIAH
HAJI	ZEPHANIAH
HILKIAH	

```
K O D A Z M A A S E I A H Z M
A I L E A M A Z I A H U U B H
W H Z E P H A N I A H E P A A
U R I A H O P A H I A H H D I
E I M M E R A T H H Z H I A R
Z E T F E A D T A I A A N N A
R S N H R L M A I L R I E A M
A B A O A U E M R K I A H U A
D I N I R M A C A I A R A H H
A H P I N B A B H A H E S S I
I S J N I A S R C H A S O O T
O A L H B B N Z E O Y N I J U
H I U P E L E A Z A R Q N T B
E L N O A R E H P I T O P A O
J E T H A U H S I B A C H V S
```

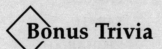

Bonus Trivia

When Lazarus came out of the grave, only his hands, feet, and face were wrapped with cloth. John 11:44

Word Search 126

HEROES OF THE FAITH

ABEL	JOEL
ABRAHAM	JONAH
AMOS	JOSEPH
BARAK	MALACHI
DANIEL	MICAH
DAVID	MOSES
ENOCH	NAHUM
ESTHER	NEHEMIAH
EZRA	NOAH
GIDEON	OBADIAH
HABAKKUK	RAHAB
HOSEA	SAMSON
ISAAC	SAMUEL
ISAIAH	SARAH
JACOB	ZECHARIAH
JEPHTHAE	ZEPHANIAH
JEREMIAH	

```
H G J P N A H U M E Z R A B V
P I V J O N A H D A B A H A R
E D N O S M A S I R H H B R I
S E J A C O B M V N A A S A M
O O R E H T S E A Z I I R K I
J N H F A M O S D N M M W B S
N H A I N A H P E Z E E X X A
M E I D J H T M A U H R U J A
A A R E H O A Y I Z E E B S C
E H A O N A E I Q C N J L A L
S T H A G O I L D Z A T E M S
O H C B I H C A L A M H I U A
H P E E B I U H S A B E N E R
K E Z L M O S E S I G O A L A
J J W P H A B A K K U K D X H
```

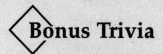

Bonus Trivia

With Nehemiah as the foreman, it took 52 days to rebuild Jerusalem's wall.
Nehemiah 6:15

Word Search 127

WOMEN OF THE BIBLE

ABAGAIL	LEAH
ADAH	LOIS
ASENATH	LYDIA
BASEMATH	MAHALATH
BATHSHEBA	MARY
BERNICE	MILCAH
BILHAH	NAAMAH
DAMARIS	PRISCILLA
DEBORAH	RACHEL
DINAH	RAHAB
ELIZABETH	REBECCA
ESTHER	RHODA
EUNICE	RUTH
EVE	SARAH
GOMER	TAMAR
HAGAR	ZILLAH
KETURAH	ZILPAH

```
C B A E F H M A H A L A T H P
A I I S P Z I L P A H R R N L
S L D T B R Q T A M A R E J E
E H Y H H E I C H T U R B L H
N A L E A A R S K R Y U E I C
A H L R E L D N C E A G C A A
T U O E V E L A I I T H C G R
H M I L C A H I I C L U A A H
S D S H A R A S Z Q E L R B L
I E E L I Z A B E T H S A A K
R B A M A R Y G T J D I N A H
A O D U R Z H T A M E S A B Q
M R O N A A M A H H G O M E R
A A H E U N I C E L O L E A H
D H R L G B A T H S H E B A Y
```

⟨ **Bonus Trivia**

Joseph, Mary, and Jesus moved to Egypt for a
while because Herod wanted to kill Jesus.
Matthew 2:13

Word Search 128

VILLIANS OF THE BIBLE

ABIRAM	HERODIAS
ABSALOM	JEZEBEL
AHAB	JUDAS
AHITHOPHEL	KORAH
AMALEK	NIMROD
AMNON	OMRI
ATHALIAH	PHAROAH
BALAAM	RABSHAKEH
CAIAPHAS	SANBALLAT
CAIN	SATAN
DATHAN	SENNACHERIB
ELYMAS	SHIMEI
GOLIATH	TOBIAH
HAMAN	ZEDEKIAH
HEROD	

```
Z L L J U D A S A I D O R E H
I E M I H S J H D O R M I N Y
A A H A I B O T C A I N S H B
V H H B M O L A S B A A J A E
H B P I O Q L I A A H S C I A
Y B I J T G F L T L A I A K T
D N B R S H M O A A R R I E H
A F A J E A O G N A O M A D A
T P H M R H N P J M K O P E L
H A A I A D C B H E L T H Z I
A M B Z A H H A A E Z C A D A
N A A M N O N E N L L E S M H
J L S A M Y L E R N L L B A P
H E K A H S B A R O E A E E F
Q K P H A R O A H B D S T T L
```

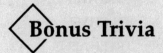

Bonus Trivia

Esau's third wife, Mahalath, was also his
cousin Ishmael's daughter. Genesis 28:9

Word Search 129

NEW TESTAMENT CONVERTS

AGABUS

AMPLIATUS

ANDREW

CARPUS

DEMETRIUS

DORCAS

EPAPHRODITUS

EUBULUS

EUODIA

FORTUNATUS

HERODIAN

JAMES

JOHN

LINUS

LOIS

LUCIUS

LUKE

LYDIA

MARK

MARY

ONESIMUS

PARMENAS

PAUL

PETER

PHILOLOGUS

PHOEBE

PUDENS

RHODA

SILAS

SOSIPATER

STACHYS

TRYPHAENA

URBANUS

```
R S D N A I D O R E H L O I S
E U O Y R E T A P I S O S Y U
T I R R S U T A I L P M A S T
E R C A P A R M E N A S P U R
P T A M I N H O J B J H L B Y
A E S Y H C A T S L I T U A P
P M U A H S S P E L I W C G H
H E T N E S A U O U C N I A A
R D A D K U U L N S B L U K E
O U N R L L O M I A N U S S N
D A U E A G R D I S B E L H A
I I T W U H N K I S E R D U W
T D R S A D O H R A E M U U S
U Y O D K S U P R A C N A F P
S L F H E B E O H P M Y O J I
```

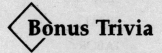

Bonus Trivia

Jonah wasn't the only prophet sent to
Ninevah. Nahum also ministered there.
Nahum 1:1

Word Search 130

HILLS AND MOUNTAINS IN THE BIBLE

ABARIM	HOREB
AMMAH	JUDAEA
BAALAH	JUDAH
BENJAMIN	JUDEAN
BETHHORON	MARS
CARMEL	MIZAR
EBAL	MOREH
GAASH	MORIAH
GALILEAN	NEBO
GAREB	OLIVES
GERIZIM	PISGAH
GILBOA	SAMARIA
GILEAD	SEIR
HACHILAH	SINAI
HALAK	TABOR
HERMON	ZION
HOR	

```
M O R I A H D O L I V E S V B
S M H A C H I L A H B P N A B
A A K S F H S H S E E J A E K
M R P K A I A T R B U L R B F
A S X M N L V A A D A O Q B F
R K M A A J G L E H H E R O M
I A I K D Q U A T A B O R Z P
A E A D U J N D E A O B L I G
G E R I Z I M I A R V M O O C
X B E N J A M I N H I B W N A
K Z P I S G A H N Z E E J S R
L Y N O M R E H A N D Z S D M
A B A R I M I R G I L E A D E
G A A S H N O R O H H T E B L
R O H N A E L I L A G X R M K
```

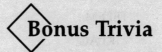

Bonus Trivia

King Jehosaphat built a fleet of trading ships that were wrecked before they ever set sail. 1 Kings 22:48

Word Search 131

CITIES OF JUDAH

ADADAH	IIM
AIN	ITHNAN
AMAM	JAGUR
BAALAH	JERUSALEM
BEALOTH	KABZEEL
BIZIOTHIAH	KASIL
DEBIR	KEDESH
DIMONAH	KINAH
EDER	LEBAOTH
EKRON	MADMANNA
ELTOLAD	MOLADAH
EZEM	SHEMA
HAZOR	SHILHIM
HEBRON	TELEM
HESHMON	ZIKLAG
HORMAH	ZIPH

```
A B E A L O T H K W M Q M Z A
B N O R K E J P A E J O H I J
I R O S I S W F L N L T E K E
Z A N O M H S E H A O L F L R
I G P Z E I T U D A T M E A U
O J I D J L E A B O M W I G S
T P E M I H H E L A A H V D A
I I A K V M D N W A M M M T E
A K B A A L A H I D A R A H M
H K G R J B A W H A N O M N S
U T S A I N Z A E H N H R A H
I U G K I B Z E A Z A G D N E
E U P K I O E K E D E S H E M
R H E B R O N D O L S M M M A
```

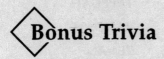

Bonus Trivia

Job had 3000 camels, at first. Job 1:3

Word Search 132

CITIES OF JUDAH #2

ADITHAIM

ADULLAM

ARAB

ASHAN

ASHNAH

AZEKAH

BOZKATH

DILEAN

EGLON

ENAM

ENGANNIM

ESHTAOL

ETHER

GAD

HADASHAH

JARMUTH

JATTIR

JOKTHEEL

KITLASH

LACHISH

LAHMAS

LIBNAH

MAKKEDAH

MIGDAL

MIZPAH

NAAMAH

RIMMON

SHAARIM

SOCOH

TAPPUAH

ZANOAH

ZENAN

ZORAH

```
G M A K I T L A S H A A R I M
W N C P A M N P B B E E M M B
N O L G E A N O L A T N I I T
C M V S H K Z J A R H A Z A L
E M G S M K Z O C A E M P H X
N I A T A E O K H G R P A T F
G R D T G D R T I J U N H I E
A H H H A A A H S A H A A D S
N Y T N D H H E H T A A S A H
N L H U A S D E S T D M H D T
I A A A M E O L E I A A N U A
M D N I K R L C C R S H A L O
E G B E T E A I O A H W H L L
A I I Y Z Q Z J D H A O N A Z
X M L S A M H A L G H Y D M F
```

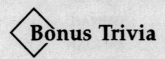

Bonus Trivia

Amen means "so let it be."

Word Search 133

MORE CITIES OF JUDAH

ACZIB	JEZREEL
ANAB	JOKDEAM
ANIM	JUTTAH
CARMEL	KAIN
DANNAH	KEILAH
DUMEH	MAON
ELTEKON	MARESHAH
ENGEDI	MIDDIN
ESHAN	NEZIB
GILBEAH	NIBSHAN
GILOH	RABBAH
GOSHEN	SECACAH
HALHUL	SHAMIR
HOLON	TIMNAH
HUMATH	ZANOAH
JANIM	ZIOR

```
L E E R Z E J N E Z I B R A E
H H S E C A C A H A C Z I B J
E A F H G I L B E A H V C Z F
N B N U O I J L A N A B K Z Z
H B I M P L T A H G J Z E A V
M A D W I E O A N M U N I N D
N R E M K T L N A I L O L O U
E A G O A H H R N E M A A A M
H N N U U E E I M X K M H H E
S I E L G S D R H A T T U J H
O M W I H D A K I H A N N A D
G G L A I C Y N O H U M A T H
I O H M B U U H V J P B H K V
H O W E X E S H A N Z I O R S
E N A H S B I N B R I M A H S
```

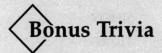

Bonus Trivia

An ephah is a dry measure of more than half a bushel. Ezekiel 45:10

Word Search 134

PRE-ISRAEL KINGS

ABIMELECH

ADONIZEDEK

AMRAPHEL

ARAD

ARIOCH

BAALHANAN

BALAK

BELA

BERA

BIRSHA

CHEDORLAOMER

EVI

HADAD

HOHAM

HORAM

HUR

HUSHAM

JABIN

JAPHIA

JOBAB

MELCHIZEDEK

OG

PHAROAH

PIRAM

REBA

REKEM

SAMLAH

SHAUL

SHEMEBER

SHINAB

SIHON

TIDAL

ZUR

```
Y J K E D E Z I H C L E M E I
D Y I S M B J A P H I A K C F
B A O N E S I H O N R E D E H
G A R G K H X Z G I D C L C N
S X B A E A F E O E H E E F A
H S R O R D B C Z E H L M X N
E H E T J A H I D P E P A F A
M I B Q L D N O A M I J H H H
E N A A M O R R I R A A S A L
B A K A D L M B A E L B U O A
E B R A A A A M K V E I H R A
R O U O L A D I T I B N C A B
H A M H U R Q J B B I R S H A
B E R A Z U R Z L U A H S P L
R H O H A M H A L M A S T C S
```

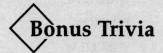

Bonus Trivia

Job's wife thought he had bad breath.
Job 19:17

Word Search 135

LEVITE CITIES

AIN	JAHZAH
ALEMETH	JATTIR
ALMON	JAZER
ANATHOTH	JOKNEAM
ANEM	KARTAH
ANER	KARTAN
ASHAN	KEDESH
BEESHTERAH	KIRJATHAIM
BEZER	LIBNAH
ELTEKEH	MAHANAIM
GEBA	MASHAL
GOLAN	MISHAL
HAMMOTHDOR	NAHALAL
HEBRON	RIMMON
HELKATH	SHECHEM
HESHBON	TABOR
HILEN	

```
U F F H E K E T L E P A T B B
M I A H T A J R I K L B N V R
T N A L O G J H E M M E A I A
H A N B I L O M O Z L G T J O
M A S H A L K N E H A T R A K
D H A N E M N N L H A J A H R
L Z A Z B M E Z O J C X K Z I
L A B M H R A A H B R E N A M
A B H H M T M H N E H N H H M
L E N S E O E K A A L S I S O
A Z A E I B T M E N T K E A N
H E H Z L M R H E D A H A H B
A R S R P I Z O D L E I O T Q
N T A B O R H C N O A S M T H
B E E S H T E R A H R P H L H
```

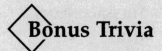

Bonus Trivia

Shem, Noah's son, was the ancestor of the
Jewish people. Genesis 11:10-26

Word Search 136

BOOKS OF THE BIBLE

ACTS

AMOS

CHRONICLES

DEUTERONOMY

EPHESIANS

EZRA

GENESIS

HABAKKUK

JAMES

JOB

JOEL

JOHN

JONAH

JOSHUA

JUDGES

KINGS

LAMENTATIONS

LUKE

MARK

MATTHEW

MICAH

NAHUM

NUMBERS

OBADIAH

PETER

PHILEMON

PSALMS

REVELATION

RUTH

SONG OF SOLOMON

THESSALONIANS

TITUS

ZECHARIAH

```
S N A I N O L A S S E H T C A
I Z S R E B M U N N U D O H R
K R A M E K U K K A B A H R Z
R K J O S H U A P I J O J O E
H A I R A H C E Z S A M J N K
L S N O I T A T N E M A L I A
D H A C I M A T T H E W N C U
J O H N E R E T E P S G T L O
M M U P S A L M S E S S G E B
N O M O L O S F O G N O S S A
J O E L Y M O N O R E T U E D
W L U K E N H A N O J R T G I
R E V E L A T I O N Z R I D A
R U T H G E N E S I S H T U H
A M O S P H I L E M O N S J O
```

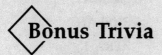

Bonus Trivia

Rhoda was the servant girl who answered the door when Peter escaped from jail.
Acts 12:13

Word Search 137

JUDAH'S PROGENY

ABINADAB

ABISHAI

ACHAR

AMMINADAB

ASHAHEL

AZARIAH

BOAZ

CALCOL

CARMI

CHELUBAI

DARA

DAVID

ELIAB

ER

ETHAN

HAMUL

HEMAN

HEZRON

JERAMEEL

JESSE

JOAB

NASHON

NETHANEEL

OBED

ONAN

OZEM

PEREZ

RADDAI

RAM

SALMA

SHELAH

ZERAH

ZIMRI

```
G  D  L  O  C  L  A  C  A  O  J  E  S  S  E
A  I  I  I  D  Q  F  B  H  B  B  D  H  T  R
R  V  O  H  A  D  B  A  R  A  I  A  E  J  O
A  A  M  A  R  B  R  O  I  A  L  S  I  B  V
D  D  G  M  Z  E  U  L  A  E  D  B  H  A  O
M  L  U  U  Z  I  E  L  H  Z  A  D  B  A  P
J  E  Q  L  O  M  R  S  E  D  U  L  A  T  I
E  H  H  P  Z  R  I  M  A  H  H  E  D  I  H
R  A  E  L  E  A  R  N  I  E  C  E  A  J  A
A  H  Z  A  M  C  I  R  M  Z  B  N  N  O  I
M  S  R  M  E  B  D  A  E  B  R  A  I  A  R
E  A  O  L  A  U  N  E  V  J  A  H  M  B  A
E  N  N  A  L  E  T  H  A  N  H  T  M  H  Z
L  X  A  S  X  P  E  R  E  Z  C  E  A  I  A
K  Z  N  U  M  K  N  O  H  S  A  N  G  C  I
```

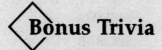

Bonus Trivia

After the Resurrection, Jesus was on the earth
for 40 days. Acts 1:3

Word Search 138

JUDAH'S PROGENY #2

ABISHUR	JETHER
AHBAN	JONATHAN
AHIJAH	MAAZ
AHLAI	MOLID
AMASA	NADAB
APPAIM	ONAM
ARDON	OREN
ASHUR	OZEM
BUNAH	PELETH
CALEB	SEGUB
EKER	SELED
HUR	SHAMMAI
ISHI	SHESHAN
JADA	SHIMMA
JAIR	SHOBAB
JAMIN	URI
JESHER	ZAZA

```
J X S D E L E S O E K E R H I
D C H B N A B H A L J Q K S A
H A I E N I M A J J A D A H S
B B M L A R D O N N J W M O A
U I M A T Z N J Z J H E D B M
G S A C D K O B I U Z A Z A A
E H S C M N A L R O V I H B P
S U W A A N S S H E S H A N E
O R N T N M H Z X H V K A W L
I O H H I I U A I M O L I D E
Z A T A A N R A R E H S E J T
N Q P K A J L M R E H T E J H
O P Z D I H I A M M A H S I Y
A K A R Y V B H Y J A I R U D
Z B U O R E N I A L H A N U B
```

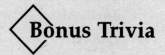

Bonus Trivia

Moses was 40 years old when he first visited
the Israelites in Egypt. Acts 7:23

Word Search 139

JUDAH'S PROGENY #3

ATTAI	MAON
BETHZUR	MARESHAH
ELEASAH	MESHA
ELISHAMA	MOZA
EPHAH	NATHAN
EPHLAL	PALET
GAZEZ	RAHAM
GESHEM	REGEM
HARAN	REKEM
HEBRON	SHALLUM
HELEZ	SHAMMAI
JAHDAI	SHEMA
JEHU	SISAMAI
JEKAMIAH	TAPPUAH
JORKOAM	ZABAD
JOTHAN	ZIPH
KORAH	

```
L A T T A I H H Y B X I M Y A
N O R B E H A H E N M U Z M R
J E P H A H P T A T L P A M M
Q O L K S I H R J L H H E A N
S W R E Z Z A E A A S H H A D
H N R K U H K H R I S A H X V
A A O R O A S O L E R T S I G
M H T A M A K E G T O M Q A J
M Z S I M S M H E J O O Z H B
A G A E H I L L U Z M E G E R
I H L E M A A C A U Z E L E H
A W M Z L P U B H M R E K E M
N A T H A N A E S I S A M A I
T J P U Y D J T A P P U A H D
P E L E A S A H L I A D H A J
```

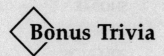

Bonus Trivia

Moses was 80 years old when he saw the burning bush. Acts 7:30

Word Search 140

JUDAH'S PROGENY #4

ABIA

ABSOLOM

ADONIJAH

AHAZ

AMNON

ASA

ATAROTH

BETHLEHEM

ELIODA

ELIPHELET

ELISHAMA

EPHRATAH

GIBEA

HAROEH

HEMATH

IBHAR

ITHREAM

JAPHIA

MACHBENA

MADMANNAH

NOGAH

OHEL

RECHAB

SHAAPH

SHEBER

SHEPHATIAH

SHEVA

SHIMEA

SHOBAB

SHOBAL

SOLOMON

TIRHANA

```
M N L A B O H S R J E F A M J
C A O E L I O D A L H R T O A
M L C M N A V F I J A N A L P
A B A H O E V P N H I O R O H
D H G N B L H E B P T N O S I
M P A L A E O I H U A M T B A
A A G J L H N S I S H A H A L
N B E E I H R A B F P G C P P
N I T R H N A I M A E M I H S
A A G X H T O T T S H A A P H
H T I F M T A D A H S C S F O
R E B E H S I M A R A L E A B
T M E H E L H T E B H G E R A
S P A H A R O E H H J P O H B
A H A Z E L I S H A M A E N O
```

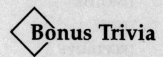

Bonus Trivia

Moses was 120 years old when he died.
Deuteronomy 34:7

Word Search 141

MORE NEW TESTAMENT CONVERTS

ANDRONICUS	OLYMPAS
AQUILA	PATROBAS
ARCHIPPUS	PERSIS
CLAUDIA	PHILEMON
CRISPUS	PRISCILLA
EPAPHRAS	QUARTUS
EUNICE	RUFUS
GAIUS	SECUNDUS
HERMES	SILVANUS
JASON	SIMON
JUDAS	THOMAS
JULIA	TIMON
JUSTUS	TIMOTHY
MNASON	TITUS
NICANOR	TROPHIMUS
NIGER	ZENAS

P C E P A P H R A S E M R E H
P H S N J U L I A S A D U J N
Q A I A O Y G B N U T I M O N
T U T L N S H U D T R G S S L
L B A R E E A T R I S A U A O
K H L R O M Z J O T N D L L F
T S L R T B O R N M N O Y J C
R A I B O U A N I U I M M R N
O L C L Y N S S C E P T I I T
P I S R V E A E U A C S N H S
H U I I K A S C S F P I O Z I
I Q R E G I N L I U U M N H S
M A P J U S T U S N A R F U R
U A I D U A L C S S T Z I L E
S G A I U S U P P I H C R A P

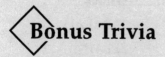

Bonus Trivia

Goliath challenged the Israelites twice a day
for 40 days before David killed him.
1 Samuel 17:16

Word Search 142

CITIES OF BENJAMIN & SIMEON

AIN	HORMAH
AMMONI	IRPEEL
ASHAN	JERICHO
BALAH	KEPHAR
BATHHOGLAH	KEPHIRAH
BETHARBAH	KIRIATH
BETHEL	MOLODAH
BETHLEBAOTH	MOZAH
BETHUL	PARAH
ELTODAD	RAMAH
ENEKKEZIZ	REKEM
EZEM	SHARUHEN
GEBA	SHEBA
GIBEON	TARALAH
HAZARSHUAL	ZELAH
HAZARSUSAH	ZEMARAIM

```
E Y H A H H D A D O T L E B B
N P A R A H H A D O L O M F E
E K M M Z N E H U R A H S G T
K E A N O H A M M O N I G H H
K P R M M L A Z R E K E M A E
E H T O A B E L H T E B Z L L
Z A L B K M G M G H O A X A U
I R A E A E J I A O R A V R H
Z I M R E E P M B S H G V A T
N S A E R P R H H E A H E T E
D I H I Z O R U I Y O S T B B
M A C E H E A I U R D N H A A
C H T T B L K I R I A T H A B
O B E T H A R B A H K H T E N
Z H A Z A R S U S A H A L E Z
```

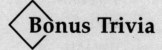

Bonus Trivia

The covering for the tabernacle was made
out of ram skins and sea cow hides.
Exodus 36:19

Word Search 143

CITIES OF ASHER & EPHRAIM

ABDON	JANOAH
ACSHAPH	KANAH
ACZIB	LIBNATH
ADDAR	LUZ
ALLAMMELECH	MISHAL
AMAD	NAARAH
APHEK	NEIEL
ATATROTH	REHOB
BETHEMEK	SHIHOR
BETIN	SHILOH
GEZER	SIDON
HALI	TAANATH
HAMMON	TAPPUAH
HEKATH	TYRE
HOSAH	UMMAH
IPHTAHEL	

```
A F H M X H B E T H E M E K A
B V T T O E C Z A Z F Z U L P
D L D L A K J R I H T A K E H
O E I L D N A N O M M A H R E
N H R G E A B H Q H P X O E K
S A S A N I M I T M A H H Z A
I T H H D N E A L O A O V E N
L H I T K D I N N U R P N G A
A P H A N E A T P H L T R A H
H I O N O P R P E A A E A Y J
Y K R A D I A Y H B H S I T Q
K P F A I T K S T O G A O I A
P D T T S B I L B E B F M H V
Z A L L A M M E L E C H A M T
H P A H S C A Y A C Z I B U U
```

◇ Bonus Trivia

Joseph's brothers didn't sell him directly to the Egyptians. They sold him to some Midianites who sold him to Potiphar in Egypt. Genesis 38:36

Word Search 144

CITIES OF ZEBULUN, ISSACHAR, & MANASSEH

BETHLEHEM	KISHION
DABERATH	MARALAH
DOR	MEGGIDO
EBEZ	NAHALAL
ENDOR	NAPHOTH
ENGANNIM	NEAH
ENHADDAH	PAZZEZ
ETHKAZIN	REMETH
HAPHARAIM	SARID
HEPHER	SBLEAM
IDALAH	SHAHAZUMAH
JAPHIA	SHIMRON
JEZREEL	SHION
KATLATH	SHUNEM
KESULLOTH	TABOR

```
S B G P N M E G G I D O V E R
H E E Z I L C B D K S S N E K
I T M H Z M A A F B I H H H Z
O H A T A J L L L D A P A R E
N L N O K A S E A D E P S O Z
J E A L H L A H D H H Z A D Z
A H P L T M E A I A A P R N A
P E H U E H H E R M S N I E P
H M O S R Q A A R U R L D H H
I H T E V E I E Z Z R O B A T
A K H K O M M F N A E Y N L A
N O I H S I K E G H R J Z A L
M I N N A G N E T A D H E R T
R R S H U N E M Q H O T B A A
D A B E R A T H O S R N E M K
```

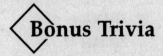

Bonus Trivia

People weren't given permission to eat meat until after the Flood. Genesis 9:3

Word Search 145

CITIES OF NAPHTALI & DAN

ADAMAH	HUKKOK
AIJALON	IRON
ASNOTH	ITHLAH
BENEBARAK	JEHUD
DAN	KEDESH
EDREI	KINNERETH
EKRON	LAKKUM
ELON	MEJARKON
ELTEKEH	RAKKATH
ENHAZOR	RAKKON
ESHTAOL	RAMAH
GATHRIMMON	SHAALABBIN
GIBBETHON	ZER
HAMMATH	ZIMNAH
HAZOR	ZORAH
HOREM	

```
V P A I J A L O N K Y Z E R E
Z O D E H A M M A T H H K A K
X G A N S N H M T Z A M O K R
L I M H N S O T V A R E K K O
G B A A K C H K E L O R K O N
A B H Z R A E A R R Z O U N H
T E T O N D R L A A E H H N S
H T Q R D A N A T L J N K O E
R H H A L H T I B E A E N R D
I O A Z I M N A H E K B M I E
M N D Z L A K K U M N E B Q K
M O O U O L O A T H S E H I G
O L Z Q H R A S N O T H B H N
N E L V F E B H T A K K A R Q
H I E R D E J H A M A R T O N
```

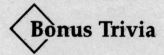

Bonus Trivia

Cain built the first city. Genesis 4:17

Word Search 146

PARABLES OF JESUS

FIG TREE	RECKONING
FRUIT	RICH FOOL
GOOD SAMARITAN	SEED
GUEST	SHEEP
LAMP	SOWER
LOST COIN	SUPPER
LOST SHEEP	TENANTS
MANAGER	TREASURE
MUSTARD SEED	TWO SONS
NARROW DOOR	UNJUST JUDGE
NET	VINEYARD
PEARL	WEEDS
PRODIGAL	YEAST
PUBLICAN	

```
R E G A N A M I N A S Z C S N
U V L O O F H C I R R S R R A
N K S T N A N E T B N R E E T
J P R O D I G A L O U C R B I
U S H E E P H O S X K D O M R
S Y W S S H S O T O R T O U A
T G U E S T W R N A I O D S M
J S E F C T E I Y U P K W T A
U D U O I A N E R T U I O A S
D D I P S G N F S V B R R R D
G N A U P I T A F H L E R D O
E D R R V E E R P J I W A S O
P E A R L Y R A E M C O N E G
L O S T S H E E P E A S L E K
T S D E E W N E T G N L J D M
```

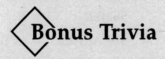

Bonus Trivia

Cain committed the first murder. Genesis 4:8

Word Search 147

JESUS' GENEALOGY #1

ADDI	JUDAH
AMOS	LEVI
COSAM	MAATH
ELIAKIM	MATTATHA
ELIEZER	MATTATLIAS
ELMADAM	MATTHAT
ER	MELEA
ESLI	MELKI
HELI	MENNA
JANNAI	NAGGAI
JOANAN	NAHUM
JODA	NERI
JONAM	RHESA
JORIM	SEMEIN
JOSECH	SHEALTIEL
JOSEPH	SIMEON
JOSHUA	TERUBBAHEL

```
E S L I H P E S O J O R I M Q
A R A H J A H T A T T A M D A
J O A N A N A R M I V E L D S
G S S T N D B U H A X R O K A
U R S T N E U I H E S J C Q I
Y E T J A T M J K S S O M A L
N Z S M I H E H E L O A C L T
I E Y H A I T R E U E J L I A
E I I N E N A T U L H M U A T
M L B R A A O G A B I T D L T
E E H Z E H L J G M B D A U A
S I M E O N U T T A I A E A M
M E L E A K X M I H N R H E M
E L I A K I M H C E S O J E E
H G M A D A M L E L L U U Z L
```

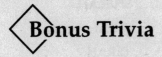

Bonus Trivia

Noah planted the first vineyard. Genesis 9:20

Word Search 148

JESUS' GENEALOGY #2

ABRAHAM	METHUSELAH
ADAM	NAHOR
AMMINADAB	NAHSHON
ARPHAXAD	NATHAN
BOAZ	NOAH
CAINAN	OBED
DAVID	PELEG
EBER	PEREZ
ENOSH	RAM
GOD	SALMON
HEZRON	SERUG
ISAAC	SETH
JACOB	SHELAH
JESSE	SHEM
KENAN	TERAH
LAMECH	

```
A G A H E N Z D Q N A H O R S
M Z M R V N O E A G E L E P K
M C U H P L O H H V H Q N P E
I A Y U A H T S S A I A V E N
N A T T A L A S H H L D R R A
A S X D E C E X A S A E H E N
D I A C A R N S A B E N H Z T
A M W I U H L O U D R T G S N
B H N G E R R N M H I A H O U
E A C Z N E P E O L T Y H D D
N A R E B A S B B A A E K A K
L O M E M S T H O D H S M D M
N L A E E A V H C A E G K Z L
M A R J H K L D A K Z B D P N
A X C I S S Q A J N I B O G J
```

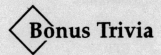

Bonus Trivia

Abel was the first shepherd. Genesis 4:2

Word Search 149

SPIRITUAL GIFTS & FRUIT
AND THOSE WHO POSSESS THEM

DEACON	KNOWLEDGE
DISCERNMENT	LOVE
ELDER	MERCY
ENCOURAGER	MIRACLES
EVANGELIST	PEACE
FAITH	PRAISE
FAITHFULNESS	PROPHECY
GENTLENESS	PROPHET
GIVER	RIGHTEOUSNESS
HEALING	SELF CONTROL
HELPER	TEACHER
HOPE	TONGUES
JOY	WISDOM

```
O H O R K N O W L E D G E O P
S O H E L P E R M S P H I R E
B P T G S I N E L S L G S I F
H E S A B I R Q J E O M S G A
E M I R J C A U O N R D E H I
A I L U Y X Q R Y L T I N T T
L R E O V I E T P U N S E E H
I A G C U D O R J F O C L O X
N C N N L N O P Q H C E T U M
G L A E G P R M N T F R N S P
I E V U H O O O J I L N E N E
V S E E P D C C L A E M G E A
E S C H S A Z O M F S E Q S C
R Y E I E Q V Y C U C N Z S E
R T W D T E A C H E R T Y S W
```

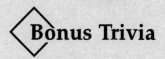

Bonus Trivia

Cain was the first farmer. Genesis 4:2

Word Search 150

AREAS OF JESUS' MINISTRY

BETHANY

BETHLEHEM

BETHSAIDA

CANA

DECAPOLIS

EMMAUS

GADARA

GALILEE

GENNESARET

GERASA

GETHSEMANE

GOLGATHA

JERICHO

JERUSALEM

JORDAN

JUDEA

KHERSA

MAGADAN

NAIN

NAZARETH

OLIVET

SAMARIA

SIDON

SYCHAR

TABOR

TYRE

```
A A N Y N A H T E B Y C T D G
E I G H T E R A Z A N A H G O
D H G A D A R A E F E S H E L
U S U D D N A N P X R A M N G
J R S E T I A S O X S R A N A
E O O C Y E A I R D N E G E T
N B H A R E N S N E I G A S H
A A C P E L Z I H J H S D A A
M T I O L I V E T T O K A R W
E S R L I L B U D O E R N E K
S U E I B A Q F R F C B D T C
H A J S K G S G A S Y C H A R
T M B E T H L E H E M P N K N
E M G V A I R A M A S A Q Z W
G E M E L A S U R E J Q T W G
```

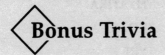

Bonus Trivia

Abram was the first Hebrew. Genesis 13:14

Word Search 151

PAUL'S MISSIONARY JOURNEYS

APPOLONIA

ASSOS

ATHENS

ATTALIA

BEREA

CENCHREA

CNIDUS

DAMASCUS

DELPHI

DERBE

EPHESUS

ISSUS

LYSTRA

MALTA

MITYLENE

MYRA

NEAPOLIS

PATARA

PHYRGIA

RHEGIUM

ROME

SALMONE

SAMOTHRACE

SARDIS

SIDON

SMYRNA

TARSUS

THESSALONICA

THYATIRA

TROAS

TYRE

```
E J S U S E H P E S U D I N C
C E N C H R E A R H E G I U M
T S J E N O M L A S W R X Y S
A H N A A A P A I L A T T A W
P T E E I R N E A P O L I S I
H E L S H N I H P L E D K E S
Y R N A S T O T I C H D E R M
R D C E M A A L A S Q Y A Y Y
G W A A L D L R O Y S D R T R
I N R M E Y H O S P H U T S N
A Y D R A T T S N U P T S I A
M R B E O S O I I I S A Y D O
Y E R M M S C X M D C C L R E
N E A T S O E U T R O A S A L
B S P A T A R A S C A N Y S W
```

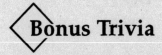

Bonus Trivia

"Apple of your eye" is hardly a new
expression. Solomon said it in Proverbs 7:2.

Word Search 152

BODIES OF WATER

ADHAIM	HALUS
ADREA	JABBOK
AEGEAN	JORDON
AQABA	KINNERATH
ARNON	LITANI
BALIKH	MEROM
BESOR	PKARPAR
BITTER	SALT SEA
CASPIAN	SHIHOR
CHERITH	TIGRIS
DAMASCUS	URNIA
DIYALA	VAN
EUPHRATES	YARMUK
GALILEE	ZAB
GREAT SEA	ZERED
HABOR	

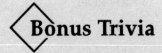

H	N	T	H	S	U	T	R	O	H	I	H	S	P	J
K	O	R	L	K	A	B	A	Q	A	B	T	W	K	O
I	N	E	A	O	E	L	S	V	E	O	A	J	A	R
L	R	T	E	B	U	Y	T	S	B	H	R	R	R	D
A	A	T	S	B	P	A	O	S	H	K	E	I	P	O
B	L	I	T	A	H	R	Q	H	E	H	N	E	A	N
I	A	B	A	J	R	M	S	S	A	A	N	E	R	Q
N	Y	C	E	K	A	U	U	I	D	B	I	L	N	M
A	I	A	R	C	T	K	C	R	R	O	K	I	A	P
T	D	S	G	H	E	M	S	G	E	R	W	L	E	P
I	S	P	D	E	S	I	A	I	A	O	U	A	G	M
L	U	I	E	R	R	A	M	T	I	Z	X	G	E	I
A	L	A	R	I	X	H	A	R	N	J	A	R	A	I
N	A	N	E	T	F	D	D	K	R	B	O	B	Z	D
N	H	L	Z	H	V	A	N	P	U	M	D	O	N	G

◇ Bonus Trivia

The Sabbath was measured from evening of
one day to the evening of the next.
Leviticus 23:32

Word Search 153

FOODS & SPICES

ALMONDS	LENTILS
APPLE	LOCUSTS
BARLEY	MANNA
BREAD	MEAT
CAKES	MILK
CINNAMON	OIL
CORN	OLIVES
CURDS	ONIONS
EGG	POMEGRANATES
FIGS	POTTAGE
FISH	PULSE
GARLIC	QUAIL
GOAT	RAISINS
GRAPES	SAFFRON
HONEY	SALT
LAMB	VENISON
LEEKS	VINEGAR

```
C G G E C F M G S K E E L N T
I I A H I Q E E L P P A V N L
V S L R N H Q U A I L R R B A
L L M R N F I S H T A O L N S
A I O B A R L E Y I C L O E Y
M T N K M G G S S U O R S E E
B N D U O K N I R C F L N G K
O E S I N O N D U F U O A L T
S L U C I S S S A P H T I D T
W X I N I G T S E W T M X L A
C U O V Q S G N N O F L V U O
A V I N E G A R P S G I F Y G
K V E N I S O N Y S E P A R G
E E O Z A N N A M B B R E A D
S U Q P O M E G R A N A T E S
```

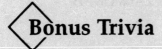
Job was the first recorded person to say "the skin of my teeth." Job 19:20

Word Search 154

ENCAMPMENTS IN THE WILDERNESS

ABARIM	MIGDOL
ALUSH	MITHKAH
BENEJAAKAM	MOSEROTH
DIBONGAD	NEBO
DOPHKAH	OBOTH
ELIM	PUNON
ETHAM	RIMMONPEREZ
EZIONGEBER	RISSAH
HASHMONAH	RITHMAH
HAZEROTH	SHEPHER
HOR	SIN
HORHAGIDGAD	SINAI
IYIM	TERAH
KEHELATHAH	ZALMONAH
LIBNAH	ZIN
MARAH	

```
H T O R E S O M S F I A N I S
A T R I S S A H O H X F P I F
L K E Z I O N G E B E R U Y N
U E T H A M W N A L O P G I I
S M I T H K A H I C I T H M S
H W H A N O M L A Z S M H E G
R T Y R I M M O N P E R E Z R
D I B O N G A D M L M A R A H
R D T E R A H N H A N B I L T
L O R H H O R H A G I D G A D
O P C N M K E H E L A T H A H
D H I O M A K A A J E N E B O
G K H N X V H T O R E Z A H B
I A O U H A S H M O N A H G E
M H R P A A B A R I M M D C N
```

Bonus Trivia

Eglon, king of Moab, was so fat that when
Ehud stabbed him with a one and a half foot
long sword, the handle sank into his belly.
Judges 3:22

Word Search 155

SOLOMON'S TEMPLE

ARK	HOUSE
BASINS	JACHIN
BLUE	LAMPSTAND
BOWLS	LINTEL
CEDAR	MINISTER
CENSERS	MOLTEN
CHAINS	OLIVE
CHERUBIM	ORACLES
CLOUD	PILLARS
COURT	PORCH
CRIMSON	PRIESTS
CYMBALS	PSALTERIES
FILLED	SHOVELS
FLOOR	SINGERS
GLORY	SNUFFERS
HARPS	

O	N	X	C	P	S	A	L	T	E	R	I	E	S	S
A	L	C	D	N	O	S	M	I	R	C	G	Z	S	Q
E	P	I	E	E	S	X	L	I	N	T	E	L	R	I
B	N	R	V	N	L	H	A	R	P	S	H	M	E	G
O	V	I	I	E	S	L	O	R	Y	P	M	I	G	L
D	C	F	H	E	C	E	I	V	K	B	I	B	N	O
C	N	E	L	C	S	P	R	F	E	S	N	U	I	R
Y	P	A	D	O	A	T	I	S	E	L	I	R	S	Y
M	M	T	T	A	O	J	S	L	C	F	S	E	R	S
B	O	R	P	S	R	R	C	H	L	C	T	H	E	N
A	L	U	O	V	P	A	I	X	O	A	E	C	F	I
L	T	O	R	E	R	M	L	V	U	U	R	W	F	S
S	E	C	C	O	T	M	A	N	D	X	S	S	U	A
B	N	X	H	S	L	Y	Q	L	B	L	U	E	N	B
S	N	I	A	H	C	B	O	W	L	S	W	O	S	X

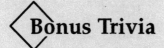

Bonus Trivia

When Abraham told people that Sarah was his sister, he was only half lying. They had the same father. Genesis 20:12

Word Search 156

SOLOMON'S TEMPLE #2

ALTAR

BOAZ

BRASS

CAPITALS

CHAMBERS

DOOR

FIR

FLOWERS

GOLD

HOOKS

INCENSE

KNOPS

LAVERS

LEVITES

LINEN

OXEN

PALM

POMEGRANATES

POSTS

POTS

POTSTABLES

PURPLE

SEA

SHOWBREAD

SILVER

SPOONS

STAVES

STONES

TIMBER

TONGS

VEIL

WINGS

```
S S M N E N I L E V I T E S L
S P N N Q C A P I T A L S I B
E G O O Z S Y B T I M B E R O
A Y N N O E T P T M L I N O A
V V Q O K P M S N Y A L O M Z
F V Z D T G S G O K P Q T W Q
S R E W O L F N U P M R S P E
S C I D O O R I S I L V E R L
R S T O P N S W P C L I E V P
E E S N E C N I N E X O R U R
V B R A S S H O W B R E A D U
A R C H A M B E R S S D T E P
L P O T S T A B L E S T L Q V
S E T A N A R G E M O P A O R
F I R S T A V E S H O O K S G
```

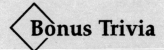

Bonus Trivia

Jerusalem was once called Jebus.
Judges 19:10

Word Search 157

OFFENSIVE & DEFENSIVE WEAPONRY

ARROWS	PIT
AXE	PITCHER
BREASTPLATE	PRAYER
CHARIOT	RIGHTEOUSNESS
DAGGER	ROD
DARTS	SALVATION
FAITH	SHIELD
FIRE	SLING
HAMMER	SNARE
HELMET	SPEAR
JAVELIN	STAVE
JAWBONE	STICK
MATTOCK	STONES
MILLSTONE	SUN
NAIL	SWORD
NET	TORCHES
PILLARS	TRUTH

```
E T A L P T S A E R B A E J Y
R K H T I A F A L S T O N E S
I C H D Y M I L L S T O N E R
G I T O R C H E S V L R O D E
H T U R T N M S P E A R C W G
T S T O U A P I H B X T E N G
E J O S K I E I E D C P I H A
O A I P G C N J L R R M I O D
U V R I T S O S M L E O Z T N
S E A T P L B T E D A M W I U
N L H C R I W R T C L R M S N
E I C H A N A A S A N E S A F
S N J E Y G J D D Y M X I E H
S F I R E E E V A T S L X H J
M X A R R O W S U E R A N S S
```

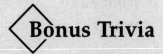

Bonus Trivia

Solomon had 12,000 horses. 1 Kings 10:26

Word Search 158

BIRDS & REPTILES

BUZZARD	OSSIFRAGE
CHAMELEON	OSTRICH
CUCKOW	OWL
DOVE	PEACOCK
DRAGON	PIGEON
EAGLE	QUAIL
FALCON	RAVEN
GLEDE	SEAGULL
HAWK	SNAKE
HERON	SPARROW
HOOPOE	STORK
KITE	SWALLOW
LAPWING	SWAN
LEVIATHON	TORTOISE
LIZARD	TURTLE
OSPREY	

```
P X H K J I N O E L E M A H C
H O X E I X D T E L T R U T I
H A W K R T P R O D R A Z I L
Z L O R R O E A A R L I A U Q
L D R A G O N V P Z T S W A N
H G R E L G A E G E Z O X N T
C L A C V K T N E N A U I R V
I E P J R F I G O B X C B S L
R D S O A W A H W L A C O W E
T E T L P R T O O L N U O C V
S S C A F A L O S U O C H P K
O O L I I L D P P G E K A N S
N C S V A J O O R A G O Q W H
X S E W R T V E E E I W D I O
O L S S D O E P Y S P U J K T
```

◇ **Bonus Trivia**

The four rivers in the Garden of Eden were
Pishon, Gihon, Tigris, and Euphrates.
Genesis 2:11-14

Word Search 159

MAKING THE TABERNACLE

ALMONDS	LINEN
ALTAR	LOOPS
ARK	MERCYSEAT
BLUE	NEEDLEWORK
BOARDS	OIL
BOWLS	PILLARS
BRANCHES	PINS
BRASS	RING
CHAPITERS	SCARLET
COURT	SHITTIM
FLOWER	SILVER
GATE	SNUFFER
GOATHAIR	SOCKETS
GOLD	STAVES
GRATE	TABLE
LAMPS	TACHES
LAMPSTAND	VEIL
LAVER	

```
G C S I S S R E T I P A H C S
A O O S T E K C O S I W D D
T U A P I N S R E W O L F N N
E R N K K A A K S L W O B A O
B T L R R H R E V L I S N T M
S S I O A T S P O O L U E S L
H N E W G R A T E L I O N P A
I U V E Y T I E S A A S I M S
T F B L U E A A S C L M L A E
T F K D K N P C H Y A T P L V
I E R E V A L T H T C R A S A
M R G E Y T A B L E A R L R T
V I O N S D R A O B S O E E S
V N L N F P I L L A R S G M T
N G D R O P S E H C N A R B H
```

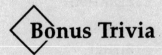

Bonus Trivia

Isaac was 40 years old when he married
Rebekah. Genesis 25:20

Word Search 160

LEVI'S PROGENY #1

AARON	KORAH
ABIASAPH	LIBNI
ABIHU	MAHLI
ABISHUA	MERAIOTH
AMRAM	MERARI
ASSIR	MISHAEL
BUKKI	MOSES
ELEAZER	MUSHI
ELIEZER	NADAB
ELKANAH	NEPHEG
ELZAPHAN	SHIMEI
GERSHOM	UZZI
GERSHON	UZZIEL
HEBRON	ZERAHIAH
ITHAMAR	ZICHRI
IZHAR	ZITHRI
KOHATH	

```
G U Z Z I K K U B H I Z U A F
E L I E Z E R G E T I Z M R P
G E H P E N M B H T Z R F I M
E L E A Z E R A H I A H Z S I
Q N P K R O M R E M O S E S D
H P A A N A I L K S I S N A Z
P L R H R O A E W O H Z W V I
A I O H P U R M L B H I H U C
S B V C H A M A A K A A M A H
A N K S U O Z K A H A D T E R
I I I H H M D L C X L N A H I
B B I S U W Y Z E I Z I A N V
A B R S F Y L E A H S I M H E
A E H T O I A R E M H A R O K
G I U Z E N O H S R E G M I N
```

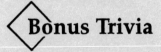

Bonus Trivia

Jericho was the City of Palms. Judges 1:16

Word Search 161

LEVI'S PROGENY #2

ABIAH	JOEL
AHIMOTH	MAHATH
AMASAI	MALCHIAH
ASAIAH	MICHAEL
ASAPH	NAHATH
ASSIR	SAMUEL
BAASEIRAH	SHEMUEL
BERACHIAH	SHIMEA
EBIASAPH	TAHATH
ELIAB	TOAH
ELIEL	UZZA
ETHNI	VASHNI
HAGGIAH	ZEPHANIAH
HEMAN	ZOPHAI
JEROHAM	ZUPH

```
H A R I E S A A B G T A I R A
H H Y M I C H A E L Y O U M L
A S A F Y Z T A H A T H A E G
I A V I J E R O H A M S U H E
H M E A B N B Q X M A M N T H
C U H M S A M B A I E A H Z P
A E T A I H L T Q H H N D Y A
R L O L H H N M S A I A N A S
E H M C A L S I T O E Z D S A
B E I H G Z E H Q A W Z Q S I
L M H I G O N M R H P U Z I B
E A A A I P H T A H A M I R E
I N N H A H H A I N A H P E Z
L H M K H A B B A I L E O J X
E H O S I I M A S A I A H F M
```

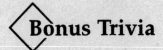

Bonus Trivia

Abraham had two nephews named Uz and
Buz. Genesis 22:21

Word Search 162

JEWISH KINGS

ABIJAH	JEHU
AHAB	JORAM
AHAZ	JOSIAH
AHAZIAH	JOTHAM
AMAZIAH	MANASSEH
AMON	MENHEM
ASA	NADAB
AZARIAH	OMRI
BAASHA	PEKAH
DAVID	PEKAHIAH
ELAH	SAUL
HEZEKIAH	SHALLUM
HOSHEA	SOLOMON
JEHOAHAZ	TIBNI
JEHOIACHIN	ZECHARIAH
JEHOIAKIM	ZEDEKIAH
JEHOSHAPHAT	ZIMRI

```
B L M A H P P B A A S H A Q J
A E U H E S H H A J I B A E N
D L L A S A A M A R O J H O D
A A L Z S H I U Z J F O M A I
N H A I A A R H V E A O I C R
N A H A N I A E Y H L P K Q M
J I S H A R H J A O D O A A I
H K H H M A C Z S S H D I M Z
A E A C A Z E M O H A I O A H
I Z M S A A Z T M A I V H Z O
H E A A H I I V E P K A E I S
A H D A H B O C N H E D J A H
K V B C N T P H H A D K A H E
E L J I R M O M E T E M K K A
P J O S I A H J M J Z N O M A
```

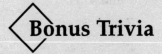

Bonus Trivia

The Israelites ate manna for 40 years until
they finally settled in Canaan. Exodus 16:35

Word Search 163

LEVI'S PROGENY #3

ABDI

ADAIAH

AHIMAAZ

AHITUB

AMARIAH

AMAZIAH

AMMINADAB

AMZI

AZARIAH

BANI

ETHAN

HASHABIAH

HILKIAH

IDDO

JAHATH

JEATERAI

JEHOZAK

JOAH

JOHANAN

KISHI

MALLUCH

SERAIAH

SHALLUM

SHAMER

SHIMEI

ZADOK

ZERAH

ZIMMAH

ZIMNAH

```
I H A S H A B I A H W J I X U
H H A I R A Z A D A D A H Z Z
Y T J E H O Z A K B R L I A N
A M A H A I A D A E A M S H H
M G Z H X C S Z T I N L E I A
A M V G A H Y A I A A L T T I
Z A K O A J E D H A N Y C U K
I L R L T J S O S M A T A B L
A L L E A Y H K I M H E M I I
H U H S M H R A K I O T Z N H
M C K A H A I O I N J H E A R
O H I R O I H M D A Q A R B S
L J Z Y J J M S A D R N A Y N
H A M M I Z B E J A I E H O F
A M A R I A H Z I B Z Q S R C
```

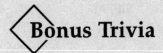

Bonus Trivia

Joash was a mere seven years old when he became king. 2 Chronicles 24:1

Word Search 164

GIANTS & OTHER ENEMIES OF ISRAEL

AHIMAN	ISHBIBENOB
AMALEK	JEBUSITES
AMMON	KADMONITES
AMORITES	KENIZITES
ANAK	LAHMI
ARBA	MIDIAN
AVVITES	MOAB
BABYLON	OG
CANAAN	PERIZZITES
EDOM	PHILISTIA
EGYPT	SAPH
GESHUR	SHESHAI
GOLIATH	SIDON
HITTITES	SIPPAI
HORITES	SYRIA

```
G S C I Z S E T I Z Z I R E P
S E T I R O M A H I M A N N T
T T A C A N A A N S V I O I S
S I P P A I X P V V A M S A Z
S Z A M A L E K I H M H P B M
E I G N P F M T S A B H O G J
T N O S S I E E O I N H B A G
I E L P D S H T B O I C I A E
S K I I J S N E D T G T H G S
U K A D M O N I T E S O Y B H
B N T O L O S I I I R P S A U
E N H Y B A T M L I T Y M O R
J F B P B E H I T X R S O M S
Q A Q R S A H E S I A M D L W
B H A F L P S K A N A H E X G
```

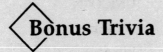

Bonus Trivia

The Sea of Galilee is also called the Lake of Gannesaret. Luke 5:1

Word Search 165

ANIMALS IN THE BIBLE

BEAR	LAMB
BITTERN	LION
BULL	LIZARD
CAMEL	MOLE
CATTLE	MOUSE
CHAMOIS	OWL
CONEY	OX
DEER	PIG
DOG	PYGARG
DONKEY	RAM
EAGLE	ROEBUCK
FERRET	SNAIL
FOX	TORTOISE
GOAT	UNICORN
HARE	WEASEL
HART	WHALE
HINDS	WOLF
HORSE	

```
V V U E E S U O M E L O M L U
F Q C E K N N O R A M R O K N
E B L O S C R E L E M A C X Y
R V P E N R U E D O N K E Y R
R P P E S E O B T J H L X T A
E I Y E Q A Y H E T W I L M E
T G G L O B E T A O I Y N U B
U C A T I M R W H E R B D D B
N L R T Q A K S O S S T R W S
R I G A H L U O I I A P A H R
O A D C C D W N X O L K Z A L
C N O O E V O O G T M H I L W
I S G E F P L I I R U A L E O
N S R A X O F L P O Y R H G R
U E L G A E X H F T H E M C J
```

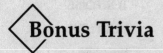

Bonus Trivia

Og, the king of Bashan, had an iron bed 13
feet long and 6 feet wide. Deuteronomy 3:11

Word Search 166

UNCLEAN FOOD SOURCES

BAT	LIZARD
CAMEL	MOLE
CHAMELEON	MOUSE
CONEY	OSPREY
CORMORANT	OSSIFRAGE
CUCKOO	OWL
EAGLE	PELICAN
FERRET	RAVEN
GIER EAGLE	SNAIL
GLEDE	SNAKE
HARE	STORK
HAWK	SWAN
HERON	SWINE
KITE	TORTOISE
LAPWING	VULTURE
LITTLE OWL	WEASEL

```
K E K A N S Y K R O T S E Q I
E C T A B E V O G L R A D N C
L O G T R U O N I D A A E A H
G R S P L K I A R B V D L W A
A M S T C W N A E W E R G S M
E O U U P S Z Y H L N R J G E
Q R C A L I T T L E O W L I L
E A L I L N W H H N Y M B E E
M N R H O E A X R I E J E R O
O T G R A R M C E W N J T E N
U H E S E W O A I S O D I A J
S H E W T X K M C L C R K G Y
E L O L W O T E R R E F W L K
T O R T O I S E U F L P K E I
W S H K E G A R F I S S O U C
```

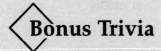

Bonus Trivia

It took Solomon 13 years to build his palace. It only took him seven years to build the temple. 1 Kings 6:38-7:1

Word Search 167

WELLS, SPRINGS & POOLS IN THE BIBLE

BEER	LOWER
BETHESDA	MARAH
BETHLEHEM	NEPHTOAH
DRAGON	OLD
ELIM	REHOBOTH
ENHAKKORE	SAMARIA
ESEK	SERPENTS
GIBEON	SHEBA
GIHON	SHEBAH
HAROD	SILOAH
HEBRON	SILOAM
ISRAEL	SIRAH
JACOBS	SITNAH
KINGS	TOWERS
LAHAIROI	UPPER

```
T O W E R S Y O S B O C A J A
E A B M G O M E H E L H T E B
S C W I J L S N O G A R D Q E
N H H L N D H S I R A H E V H
Q O E E A H A O L I S N D I S
N M I B I S R A E L H K E S E
F S A M A R I A R A Z N K S A
H T O B O H E R K H E E I E U
S S I L O A M K N A R P N R S
H U A N M N O E O I E H G P I
A S K K N R H H E R W T S E T
R A D S E H T E B O O O E N N
O N O R B E H E I I L A Q T A
D M C I R E E B G H Z H T S H
H A R A M C L Y R E P P U R V
```

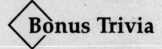

Bonus Trivia

Three o'clock in the afternoon was
prayertime in Paul's day. Acts 3:1

Word Search 168

GENTILE STRONGHOLDS

ADMAH

ARABIA

ARPHAD

ASSYRIA

BELA

BOZRAH

CALNO

CHALDEA

CHITTIM

CUSH

DEDAN

DUMAH

ELAM

ELLASAR

GOG

GOMER

GOMORRAH

HAMATH

IDUMEA

KEDAR

KIR

LIBYA

LUD

MEDIA

NINEVAH

NOPH

PERSIA

PHUT

SEPHARVAIM

SHINAR

SODOM

SYRIA

TEMA

TYRUS

ZEBOIIM

ZIDON

ZOAN

```
R G D E D A N A T U H P H G M
W G O M E R Z P S K I R P O I
H M P G P N A E H S D G O M A
J A L E O M C S B A Y W N O V
Z Z M D R U B E A O M R L R R
T O I U S S Z A L L I D I R A
N Z A H D W I R U A L I A A H
D I L N H A M A T H M E M H P
C A N I P X H B P V C M R C E
H S H E B I T I B O Z R A H S
I C Y P V Y D A U F J E D A S
T B E R R A A U I A D Y E L O
T B E U I A H L M D M U K D D
I Z S L C A L N O E E E L E O
M U N R A N I H S L A M T A M
```

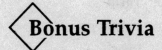

Bonus Trivia

Manna means "what is it?"

Word Search 169

MUSICAL INSTRUMENTS & PRAISE WORDS IN THE BIBLE

ALLELUIA	JUST
ALMIGHTY	OMNIPOTENT
AMEN	ORGAN
BLESSED	PIPE
CORONET	POWER
CYMBAL	PRAISE
DULCIMER	PSALTERY
FAITHFUL	PURE
FLUTE	REJOICE
GLORY	RIGHTEOUS
GRACE	SALVATION
GREAT	TABRET
HALLELUJAH	TIMBREL
HARP	TRUE
HIGH	TRUMPET
HOLY	VIOL
HONOR	VOICE
HORN	

```
C E R F D O M N I P O T E N T
Y C E X U R T A B R E T U L F
M A W A L L E L U I A N S H H
B R O E C I O V H O R N N O I
A G P M I T E N O R O C O L G
L J R S M L E R B M I T I Y H
S O A M E N P E U R T V T R T
U R H Y R E S I A R P F A O R
O G F A I T H F U L F B V L U
E A V Y T H G I M L A E L G M
T N B F H A J U L E L L A H P
H E C R E J O I C E W Y S C E
G L O I V P U R E H O N O R T
I G R E A T I P S A L T E R Y
R O T S U J H P D E S S E L B
```

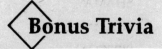

Bonus Trivia

Jacob told his sons to take pistachio nuts to
the ruler in Egypt. Genesis 43:11

Word Search 170

DAVID'S MIGHTY MEN

ABIEL	IRA
ADINA	ITHMAH
AHIAM	ITTAI
ASAHEL	JASHOBEAM
AZMAVETH	JASIEL
BANI	JERIBAI
BENAIAH	JOHA
ELHANAN	JONATHON
ELIAHBA	MAHARAI
ELIEL	MEBUNNAI
ELIPHELET	NAHARI
HANAN	OBED
HELED	PAARAI
HELEZ	SHAMA
HEZRAI	SHAMMAH
HIDDAI	SIBBECAI
HURAI	URIAH
IGAL	UZZIA
ILAI	ZALMON

```
J I X Z O M A E B O H S A J I
Q S I B B E C A I E H T B I A
H L E H A S A V L A N U H T R
V D I O I A R I M J R A A H Z
Z I J L A R P M O I H I I M E
A N A E L H A N A N E A L A H
L A B I E H A H S H L D E H H
M B I L S T B W A A E D I D I
O I E E H E L U G N D I S L G
N T L O A V S I K H L H A V X
Z L N L M A I T T A I I J A H
U A H I A M A H A R A I W N E
O J O H A Z M E B U N N A I L
J E R I B A I P A A R A I D E
O Q A I Z Z U H H U R A I A Z
```

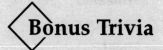

Bonus Trivia

Samson had seven braids in his hair.
Judges 16:13

Word Search 171

KING SAUL'S FAMILY

ABDON	JEHIEL
ABINADAB	KISH
AHAZ	MALCHISHUA
AHIO	MELECH
ALEMETH	MERIBBAAL
AZEL	MICAH
AZMAVETH	MOZA
AZRIKAM	NADAB
BAAL	NER
BINEA	OBADIAH
BOCHERU	REPHAIAH
ELEASAH	SAUL
ESHBAAL	SHEARIAH
GEDOR	SHIMEAM
HANEN	TAHREA
ISHMAEL	TIMRI
JARAH	ZUR

```
L U A S M A K I R Z A U E Y O
S L E O A U H S I H C L A M G
B I N E A D L L E Z A N R E H
R A L I S H M A E L E E D M A
B E E E A L I Z A N N O S L S
R A P R I B A O A B R H H A A
M L D H H H D H W L U A I A E
I E G A A A E O W A R I M B L
C M L T N I T J N A E R E H E
A E J E B I A J J B H A A S U
H T M A C T B H O B C E M E H
V H D J Q H B A M I O H N H E
C A R U Z P T B O R B S S Y W
N H A I D A B O Z E T I M R I
H T E V A M Z A A M K I R N I
```

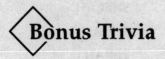

Bonus Trivia

Myrrh is a gum resin.

Word Search 172

ABRAHAM'S PROGENY

ABIDA	KEDAR
ASSHURIM	LEUMMIM
CARMI	MANASSEH
DEDAN	MEDAN
ELDAAH	MIDIAN
EPHAH	MIZZAH
EPHER	NAHATH
EPHRAIM	NEBAJOTH
ER	ONAN
ESAU	PALLU
HANOCH	PEREZ
HEZRON	SHAMMAH
ISAAC	SHEBA
ISHBAK	SHELAH
ISHMAEL	SHUAH
JACOB	ZERAH
JOKSHAN	ZIMRAN

```
C A R M I N O R Z E H J E N L
N E I S H M A E L S H E B A S
A S K O S I J O K S H A N H Z
N A E H S H M N N E E M E E M
O U U H C U A L S N D L R I Y
O A B O L I E S A X A E A H U
H A N L D U A R S H P R H A Q
K A A I M N M I I H H M C Z E
H P M M A I A G S P U E Q Z N
I Y I M Z R F H E A Q R B I E
N M T L A Z E R A H A O I M L
A B I D A H E R A T C C X M D
D P E Z R H S H W A H K B Z A
E K A C P M P V J M E D A N A
D T U E M E N E B A J O T H H
```

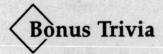

Bonus Trivia

Frankincense is a combination of gum
and spices.

Word Search 173

THREE LETTER WORDS

AVA	FOX	LAW
AWE	FRO	LAY
AWL	GAP	LUD
BAD	GAT	LUZ
BAG	GIN	MAD
CUD	HAI	NET
CUP	HAM	NEW
CUT	HAN	NOE
DAM	HAP	OAK
DAN	HEM	OAR
DEN	ICE	OFT
DIE	IIM	PAI
DOR	ILL	PAN
EHI	INK	PAU
ELI	JAH	PAW
END	JAW	PEN
ERI	JOB	RAW
ERR	KEY	RED
FIG	KIN	REI
FIR	LAD	REU
FIT	LAP	RIB

```
Y U H P A S A E O T A A I S N
W A R W O V S N X R E U S E G
P W L I A W D E A E S L W A I
E A I E R W A A W P V A I E N
H L W D N A N G B J I H R R H
I G A B U J P A O K A R T O A
N L U D R A I B H J A N E D I
M F I Z L P I T A S F O N N Z
A B I E L X S F N O E W A R D
H F I R I H K O X P M M N I T
Z M I R T R E I R K A I E K L
O U A G A T I M N F N U I E E
P C L D D C G D P D I I A Y U
A T U E E N E T A E A T P U C
G C R T R W H Y P M N N T I E
```

RID	TEN	VEX
RUN	TIE	VOW
SAP	TIL	WAG
SAT	TIN	WAR
SEA	TIP	WEN
SEM	TOE	WHY
SEW	UEL	ZER
SIA	URI	ZIA
SII	USE	ZIF

Word Search 174

ACT	EWE	KOA
ADD	EYE	LAW
AGE	FAR	LID
AGO	FAT	LIP
AHA	FEW	LOD
AIN	GET	LOP
AIR	GOB	LOT
ARK	GOD	LOW
BOW	GOG	MAN
BUD	HAY	MAT
BUY	HID	MAW
BUZ	HIN	NER
CIS	HUR	NEW
COW	HUZ	NOB
COZ	INN	NOD
CRY	IRI	NON
DRY	IRU	ONE
DUE	JEW	ONO
EAR	JOT	PIN
EAT	JOY	PIT
EVI	KIR	PUA

```
R E Z C I S U E Y E U D R U H
E W N U N N E H N U R D O S S
N O A I B A O E I T A U P U M
B T P M R T K D O N H E N A P
C E L K O R I I R A U V N G I
R G O J G N R O U O Z I I E L
Y T W S O W E N P K T Z I R U
D O L S B Y N O W R I S U P I
C W E F R R S N Y Z H I D A Z
O B U D U I I L N O N Y A H O
W B U Z G Z A I U N T C A A C
O N E Y O W A F R P S E A R G
T C F B D L A L O P W E J O M
W I T A O R D I L E I O G W A
O N O T T W D A G O W T E A T
```

PUL	SON	TWO
PUR	SOP	WIT
ROE	SOW	WOE
ROT	SUE	WON
ROW	SUN	WOT
RUN	SUP	ZIN
SEA	TOI	ZIZ
SEE	TOW	ZUR
SOD	TRY	

Word Search 175

FOUR LETTER WORDS

AGAG	HEAL	RIPE
APES	HEAR	SALT
BACA	HEED	SAVE
BULL	KILL	SEEN
BUZI	KING	SEND
COOS	KISH	SHUR
CROP	LAME	SICK
DEED	LIFE	TEIL
EVIL	LIKE	TELL
FENS	LIVE	TIME
FLAX	LORD	TRUE
FOOD	LOVE	WELL
FRAY	MEAT	WIFE
FROG	MOON	WINE
GATE	MUST	WOOD
GATH	OBEY	WORD
GONE	POOL	WORK
HATE	REAP	

```
E F I L G L L D R O L H E A R
L G O N E I W I Y T E P T C E
N O R B K E I A V A L I O A L
P G O E U T F D L E D O O W G
M N V S A L E J O M S G V I W
O I L W E P L F J O A N W E H
O K I L O E Y L D T F O I L A
N N T S I R N A E U R S G C T
E I K R E K K X R D H L A M E
C Z D C U N F A D F E B G V L
E U F E I E D K P L E Y A L E
P B U Y E S N E F E D K E M D
I E V I L D M U S T S T I B F
R U H S K O C P O R C T N S O
W E L L G O R F S A L T E X H
```

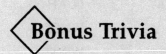

Bonus Trivia

Isaac means "he laughed."

Word Search 176

MORE FOUR LETTER WORDS

BORN	KINE	PHUT
CALF	KITE	PLEA
CARE	KNOW	POMP
COME	LAMB	PREY
CROSS	LAUD	RIOT
DEAD	LEES	ROLL
DOVE	LOAF	SHOA
FINS	LOAN	SIGN
FOOT	LOFT	SOAL
GUNI	MAII	SODI
HAFT	MASH	SORE
HILL	MIND	SOUL
HIND	MIRY	SPUE
HOLY	MOZA	SUAH
HOST	NERI	WHET
IJON	OBIL	WIND
IMLA	OMER	WOMB
ISHI	ONAM	
KEEP	PATE	

```
W Y E R O S M S X R I O T T M
I F L A C B S I X P L E A U A
N B Z Y I O M E N O P B K H N
D O K R R D T A A D Z M N P O
M R E C A I N N L A T O O F J
H N E E K S M I W L L W W P I
A M P O P S R U H M C A R E W
F A B U S U E U E I F A O L Y
T I E S H A M M T O S I Y S L
L I E H O H O P R E Y I H L O
N E O K A C D U A L Y I G S H
L S H D I S R O L L L E F N I
T B C S E N O O X L O V I W D
P A T E A A E U A H F O N X O
I N U G E M D Y L L T D S G S
```

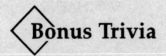

Bonus Trivia

Noah's ark had three stories. Genesis 6:16

Word Search 177

NEW TESTAMENT CONVERTS

ANANIAS	JOANNA
ANNA	JOSEPH
APELLES	JOSES
APPHIA	JUDE
ARISTARCHUS	JUNIAS
ASYNCRITUS	LEVI
BARNABUS	MARTHA
BARTHOLOMEW	NEREUS
CEPHAS	SERGIUS
CLOE	SOSTHENES
CORNELIUS	SUSANNA
CRESCENS	SYMEON
DIDYMUS	TERTIUS
HERMAS	ZACCHAEUS

```
F A A S E N E H T S O S H Z I
W P B A R N A B U S E S O J D
N E R E U S T I S U I G R E S
S B R K Y S L S U M Y D I D S
U L A M A E H C E P H A S A U
S F E R N R T E K O Q O I S T
A O T R T J I J R H L N A N I
N N O E O H L S S M A C P E R
N C N A R J O A T N A U P C C
A U N A O T I L A A T S H S N
C N S S Z N I V O H R T I E Y
A A E D U Z Z U N M T C A R S
M P I J J U D E S D E R H C A
H A S U E A H C C A Z W A U J
U I V E L A P E L L E S J M S
```

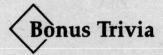

◇ Bonus Trivia

Esau was sometimes called Edom, which
means red. Genesis 25:30

Word Search 178

TRAITORS & ASSASSINS

ABIATHAR	HOSHEA
ABIMELECH	ISHMAEL
ABSALOM	JEHU
ADONIJAH	JOAB
AHITHOPHEL	JOZALIAD
ALEXANDER	JUDAS
AMASA	PEKAH
ATHALIAH	SANBALLAT
BAASHA	SHALLUM
DELILAH	SHEBA
DEMAS	SHIMEI
DIOTREPHES	TERESH
EHUD	ZABAD
HAMAN	ZIBA
HAZAEL	ZIMRI

```
N M G D R L E A M H S I T E P
I C O O I E S A M E D Y I A J
X E Z L H O D H J O A B R H O
C A M U A A T N E A U A M I Z
I D D I B S Y R A B B F I T A
A O S A H A B E E X A I Z H L
R N Z A B S H A B P E H Z O I
A I J S N I W A E A H L Q P A
H J C U A B M Z I H A E A H D
T A H O D M A E T L S S S E J
A H L A X A A L L E A O H L E
I N D I Z H S S L E R H H A H
B M U L L A H S A A C E T A U
A P D F N E E D L S T H S A N
Y H A M A N D L P E K A H H D
```

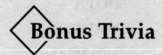

Bonus Trivia

Goliath was over nine feet tall.
1 Samuel 17:4

Word Search 179

ANGELS: NAMES, KINDS, & SEEN BY

ABADDON	JOSEPH
ABRAHAM	JOSHUA
APOLLYON	LAZARUS
BALAAM	LOT
CORNELIUS	MANOAH
DANIEL	MARY
DEVIL	MICHAEL
DRAGON	MOSES
ELIJAH	PAUL
GABRIEL	PETER
GIDEON	PHILIP
HAGAR	SALOME
ISAIAH	SATAN
JACOB	SERAPH
JESUS	SERAPHIM
JOANNA	ZECHARIAS
JOHN	

```
G Y G L T A D N A T A S M A T
M Z A I N G U A P M A B I B E
A L B V O Y J H N E J U H A M
P R R E E H P E S I T N P D O
O A I D D H P H S O E E A D L
L G E D I T Y A D H J L R O A
L A L L G R I I R P N S E N S
Y H I T A R M A A E E Y S U U
O P Z M A H A S G S S W I L A
N W S H J A A I O O H L A E B
M I C O P O L M N J E Z B A R
X E H A X N A A N N A O J H A
Z N U O Q A B A R R C P I C H
M L T O L M F O U A L C O I A
E L I J A H C S J E S U S M M
```

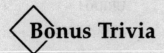

Bonus Trivia

A ten-acre vineyard will produce only a bath
of wine, or about six gallons. Isaiah 5:10

Word Search 180

BUILDERS & DESTROYERS OF ALTARS

ABRAHAM	JERUBBAAL
ABRAM	JESHUA
AHAB	JOASH
AHAZ	JOSHUA
ATHENIANS	JOSIAH
BALAK	LORD
BEZALEEL	MANASSEH
DAVID	MANOAH
GAD	MOSES
GIDEON	NOAH
HEZEKIAH	REUBEN
ISAAC	SAUL
ISRAEL	SOLOMON
JACOB	URIJAH
JEROBOAM	ZERUBBABEL

```
A J O A S H L E E L A Z E B S
U U R I J A H A Z Q B G D T N
H G I D E O N M H A I S O J A
S T G A D J H V L J L U A S I
E J V Q L I M A O B O R E J N
J J I L N B K M A R B A L E E
H A I K E Z E H U J N X E C H
L A A B B U R E J H T N B M T
A C Q U U S O T E A F S A H A
U M D M E X L S H I O H B H J
H V R S R E S A S L A A B A A
S L O C A A B A O R Q O U O C
O M L R N C A M B V H N R N O
J N S A K C O A H N G A E A B
H I M Z W N D A V I D T Z M I
```

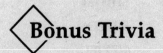

Bonus Trivia

Gideon had 71 sons. Judges 8:3

Word Search 181

JACOB'S PROGENY

AMRAM	JUDAH
ARD	LEVI
ASHER	LIBNI
BENJAMIN	MACHIR
DAN	MAHLI
EHI	MANASSEH
EPHRAIM	MUPPIM
GAD	MUSHI
ERA	NAAMAN
GUNI	NAPHTALI
HEBRON	REUBEN
HUPPIM	ROSH
ISSACHAR	SHILLEM
IZHAR	SHIMEI
JAHZEEL	SIMEON
JEZER	UZZIEL
JOSEPH	ZEBULUN

```
T A R F E P H R A I M B R M Y
M Q H P E S O J B G S I A E N
U D Y I I M H A E E H H H L E
P H R L N A J A N R I E Z L B
P I H A B C E M J A M J I I U
I A S C I H Z R A N E F L H E
M F C S L I E A M A I A H S R
I V E L A R R M I D T Z E N M
J I L M A C N W N H R H S U H
A H C L S A H U P E E H S L S
H S E D M D Z A H B J U A U O
Z U I A M Z N S R U X P N B R
E M A G I Q A O D C U P A E F
E N H E I G N A G U N I M Z H
L K L M J T H J N O E M I S Y
```

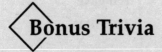

Bonus Trivia

David and Bathsheba had four children.
1 Chronicles 3:5

Word Search 182

PLACES OF ALTARS

ARARAT	MAMRE
ATHENS	MIZPEH
BEERSHEBA	MOREH
BETHEL	MORIAH
CANAAN	OPHRAH
CARMEL	RAMAH
DAMASCUS	REPHIDIM
EBAL	SAMARIA
EGYPT	SHECHEM
FIELD	SICHEM
GIBEON	SINAI
HEAVEN	TABERNACLE
HEBRON	TEMPLE
JERUSALEM	THRONE
JORDAN	ZOPHIM

H	M	I	H	P	O	Z	B	V	M	Q	X	N	G	P
A	U	D	F	B	H	H	E	R	O	M	C	A	I	M
R	P	A	Z	K	A	H	E	E	D	E	A	A	B	E
H	K	M	R	M	M	E	R	P	L	L	R	N	E	N
P	O	A	E	E	A	A	S	H	E	A	M	A	O	O
O	J	S	L	H	R	V	H	I	H	S	E	C	N	R
T	O	C	C	G	E	E	D	T	U	L	A	U	H	
P	R	U	A	E	C	N	B	I	E	R	X	R	B	T
Y	D	S	N	H	M	H	A	M	B	E	H	A	J	S
G	A	V	R	S	S	M	E	T	A	J	A	R	A	D
E	N	Y	E	G	T	I	E	P	V	M	I	A	T	L
Y	H	E	B	R	O	N	N	B	Z	U	R	T	H	E
A	I	R	A	M	A	S	S	A	A	I	O	E	E	I
E	G	U	T	S	U	R	E	P	I	L	M	Z	N	F
S	I	C	H	E	M	T	E	M	P	L	E	F	S	P

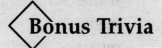

Bonus Trivia

If an Israelite stole someone's sheep, he had to pay it back with four sheep. Exodus 22:1

Word Search 183

THE WORD OF GOD IS (A) . . .

BREAD	MILK
BROAD	NIGH
COMFORT	PERFECT
COUNSELOR	PRECIOUS
DELIGHT	PROVED
ENGRAFTED	QUICK
FAITHFUL	SETTLED
HERITAGE	SHARP
JUDGEMENT	SINCERE
JUST	SONG
LAMP	SURE
LAW	SWEET
LIFE	SWORD
LIGHT	TESTIMONY
LIVING	TRIED
MEAT	TRUTH
MEDITATION	WISE

```
T N J T M G X L I F E P H J B
H T U R T T Y S D W W R E S T
G G U O K C N U E I D A R U N
I N R F T E O O T S E H I R E
L O O M E F I I F E L S T E M
E S L O S R T C A M I Q A C E
R H E C T E A E R E G G G D G
E F S H I P T R G A H L E R D
C A N G M T I P N T T G A O U
N I U I O K D A E P N G M W J
I T O N N L E T R I E D K S K
S H C W Y I M F V B R O A D C
Y F M L A M P I P B R E A D I
R U T S U J L D E L T T E S U
Z L T E E W S P R O V E D E Q
```

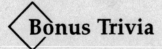

Bonus Trivia

Solomon's throne had six steps with twelve
lions sitting on them. 2 Chronicles 9:18

Word Search 184

PRAISE: WHERE, HOW, & WHY

ACTS	INSTRUMENTS
CLAP	ISLANDS
CONGREGATION	LEAPING
CREATION	LOUD
CYMBALS	MERCY
DANCE	MIGHT
EARTH	ORGANS
FIRMAMENT	SANCTUARY
FLUTES	SEAS
FOOD	SING
FOREVER	THANKSGIVING
GATES	UPRIGHTNESS
GREATNESS	VOICE
HARP	WORKS
HEIGHTS	ZION

```
T N E M A M R I F X E G B F H
J B M U A C F W J L N A L D E
T S S N P F Y O O L G U R Q I
H A N S O R R M R R T A I T G
A N S O E I I S B E K Z T L H
N C D N I N T G S A V S N E T
K T L R A T T A H P L E F A S
S U S M G G A A E T W S R P U
G A A I P S R G E R N G N I S
I R E G S R Y O E R C E I N N
V Y S H S L A C V R G L S G S
I G E T P O A H R O G A A S T
N Z I O N U D N P E I N V P C
G E C N A D D Z D F M C O L A
Q S T N E M U R T S N I E C G
```

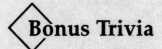

Bonus Trivia

Hosanna means "save now."

Word Search 185

PRAISE: WHO & WHAT

ANGELS	MAIDENS
BEASTS	MEN
CATTLE	MOON
CEDARS	MOUNTAINS
CHILDREN	PEOPLE
DEEPS	PRINCES
DRAGONS	ROCKS
FIRE	SAINTS
FOWL	SERPENTS
HAIL	SNOW
HANDS	STARS
HEART	SUN
HILLS	TREES
HOSTS	VAPOR
ISRAEL	WATERS
JUDGES	WIND
KINGS	

```
D N E A W A K H V A P O R P X
S X E I N S T N E P R E S B S
E A D R R G S D R A G O N S M
H J I L D P E P W W R S C S E
I U F N E L E L X D R T L K N
L D U E T O I B S A A F O F S
L G D J P S L H D J I B S U N
S E R L E W S E C R K I N G S
A S E E O T C J E M I G D S F
H W R F S N E D I A M N L E C
A T O O Z L E A R S I H L C A
N A H N S R E T A W V K A N T
D Q D L S T N O O M X B S I T
S L H S R A T S T S A E B R L
Q S N I A T N U O M H Q H P E
```

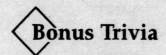

Bonus Trivia

The Israelites couldn't eat storks.
Leviticus 11:19

Word Search 186

EMOTIONS & ATTITUDES

ANGER

BITTERNESS

CONTEMPT

COURAGE

DECEIT

DESIRE

DISAPPOINTMENT

ENVY

FEAR

GREIF

GUILE

GUILT

HAPPY

HATE

HOPE

HUMILITY

JEALOUSY

JOY

LOVE

MERCY

PEACE

PRAISE

PRIDE

REJOICING

REPENTANCE

REPROACH

SHAME

SORROW

SUFFERING

TRUST

VANITY

WANT

WORSHIP

WRATH

```
A N G E R T H Y V N E A R H G
C Y R C H N T P R I D E C U S
A T E N U E A I S E S A I O D
Y I I A M M R B V I O L R F R
S N F T I T W O A R T R C E V
U A B N L N L R P E O O J G J
O V I E I I P E T W U O G U J
L U T P T O R A A R I T N I O
A P T E Y P H N A C T P I L Y
E I E R D P T G I R E M R E D
J H R R E A E N U A P E E E E
H S N A S S G S C W O T F M C
I R E E I I T E S U H N F A E
P O S F R D M E R C Y O U H I
C W S A E S H A P P Y C S S T
```

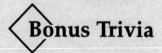

Bonus Trivia

Jesus means "the Lord saves."

Word Search 187

THE LORD IS MY . . .

BREAD	PROPITIATION
BUCKLER	PROVIDER
DELIVERER	REDEEMER
FATHER	REFUGE
FORTRESS	REWARD
GOD	ROCK
GOODNESS	SALVATION
HEALER	SAVIOUR
HELPER	SHEILD
HORN	SHEPHERD
JUDGE	SONG
KING	SUFFICIENCY
LIGHT	TEACHER
MASTER	TOWER
PEACE	VICTORY

```
X P R M H D T T R E F U G E R
N Y R E N O E R E H T A F E B
G O C O P O R L P C D W W Y E
X O I N V L I N I Z A O B V D
S R O T E I E T E V T E G I R
S S E D A I D H A G E B P C E
E R E D N I C E M V N R O T H
I E R R E E T I R A L O E O P
J L U R T E S I F V S A S R E
U A O V E R M S P F R T S Y H
D E I D E L O E S O U O E U S
G H V W A W K F R P R S C R O
E I A I R E H C A E T P N K N
N R S L V X R Q U T H G I L R
D L I E H S X B Z B G N I K Q
```

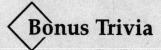

Bonus Trivia

Under David's rule, there were more than one million men who could handle a sword in Israel. 1 Chronicles 21:5

Word Search 188

HELPING OTHERS: WHO, HOW, & WHY

ABSTAIN	GIVE
ALL	GOOD
BEAR	KIND
BLESS	LABOR
BOWELS	LEND
CHILDREN	LOVE
CHRISTIANS	MERCY
CLOTHE	NEIGHBOR
COMFORT	PRAY
COMPASSION	PROPHESY
EDIFY	REAP
ENEMIES	REWARD
ESTEEM	SINNERS
EVIL	SONS
FELLOWSHIP	UNTHANKFUL
FORBEAR	WEAK
FORGIVE	

```
J C N U C N N O D R A W E R Y
E M L C L H O E A B S T A I N
W V Y O H L R I I L D E V O L
E L I C T I U I S G A N D V O
R D I G R H L F S S H B E I R
F E I V R E E D K T A B O L A
O Q A F E O M Y R N I P O R E
R B P P Y J F A S E A A M R B
B L S R E N N I S E N H N O N
E E H T R O F M O C H G T S C
A S X G O O D A Y A R P U N K
R S F E L L O W S H I P O I U
Q N S E I M E N E A L J N R O
W O E B O W E L S A L D G C P
Y S K E S T E E M M K L U Q F
```

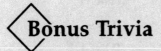

Bonus Trivia

What prophet would not declare his
prophecy until music was played?

Elisha. 2 Kings 3:15

Word Search 189

ANATOMY IN THE BIBLE

ARM	HEART
BACK	HEEL
BEARD	JOINTS
BELLY	KNEE
BLOOD	LEG
BONE	MARROW
CHEEK	MOUTH
EAR	NAVEL
EYE	NECK
FACE	NOSE
FAT	SHOULDER
FINGER	SIDE
FOOT	TEETH
FOREHEAD	THIGH
HAIR	TOE
HAND	TONGUE
HEAD	

```
F D E S O N Z E F E F B J B Z
L B A H B X B D D L H E E L L
Y L G E P F L I M A R R O W J
E L A Q H C O S M R E N O B R
U R L W H P O R E D L U O H S
D U E E T Y D G A F A C E A P
W T E H B V N F Q H B S L H S
K K N T G I T F O E E E C R Q
S C K Y F I M O L R G A U H H
J T A F Q G H T O I E Y R T N
S M Y B R H O T W F P H E T E
I Z D I A E U G N O T E E V C
E J A N Y Z M R A C T A W A K
Y H D Z L H T U O M W R S O D
E M L E V A N Y J O I N T S U
```

Bonus Trivia

If the disciples had paid for the food to feed
the 5000-plus people, it would have cost
eight month's pay. Mark 6:37

Word Search 190

JOBS & TITLES

ARMOR BEARER	LAWYER
BAKER	MASON
COMMANDER	MESSENGER
DAUGHTER	MINISTER
FATHER	PRIEST
FISHERMEN	PROPHET
HARLOT	PUBLICAN
HERDMEN	SAILOR
HUNTER	SCRIBE
HUSBAND	SHEPHERD
HUSBANDRY	SINGER
INNKEEPER	SON
JAILER	STEWARD
JUDGE	TILLER
KING	WIFE

```
N S Q S H E P H E R D M E N T
E I Q T S E I R P L A W Y E R
G N M E S S E N G E R N R S K
D G N E M R E H S I F O E R P
U E B I R C S J U Z W S K E U
J R L J A I L E R N Q A A D B
R E P E E K N N I Z T M B N L
Z L T D A U G H T E R E O A I
K P F A T H E R T Z E P R M C
W I F E Y R D N A B S U H M A
A R M O R B E A R E R T R O N
D R A W E T S A K B N O S C P
H A R L O T R R O L I A S Z T
K I N G T E H P O R P J C Z H
T I L L E R R E T S I N I M V
```

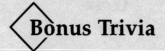

Bonus Trivia

Abba means "dear father" in Aramaic.

Word Search 191

DISASTER IN THE BIBLE

ANTICHRIST	HAIL
BEAST	LIGHTNING
BLAINS	LOCUSTS
BLOOD	MICE
BOILS	MURRAIN
CAPTIVITY	PLAGUE
DARKNESS	SCORPIONS
DEATH	SERPENTS
EARTHQUAKE	SHIPWRECK
EMERODS	SIEGE
FAMINE	SORES
FIRE	THUNDER
FLIES	TUMORS
FLOOD	ULCERS
FROGS	WAR
GNATS	

```
R S I K T H S C O R P I O N S
A D T S I R H C I T N A V F U
W A M A E V R S R O M U T R S
V R U N N I U B O I L S B O O
F K R F Y G L V E Y I S O G R
A N R L D R C F K T A H S S E
M E A O T E E G A I H I D E S
I S I O Z D R T U V Q P O R S
N S N D D N S U Q I E W R P T
E Y N O S U I E H T U R E E S
L F O I Q H E C T P G E M N U
X L I B A T G I R A A C E T C
B S C R W L E M A C L K S S O
M T S A E B B G E T P W J W L
G N I N T H G I L H T A E D U
```

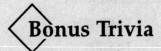

Bonus Trivia

Messiah means "anointed one" in Hebrew.

Word Search 192

CITIES EAST OF THE JORDAN

ABILA

ADAM

AROER

ATAROTH

BAALGAD

BEON

BETHNIMRAH

BETHREHOB

BETONIM

BEZER

DAN

DIBON

EDREI

GADARA

GERASA

HAM

JAZER

JOGBEHAH

KAMON

KENATH

KIRIATHAIM

LODEBAR

MACHAERUS

MAHANAIM

MEDEBA

NEBO

NIMRAH

NOBAH

PELLA

RABBA

ROGELIM

SEBAM

TABBATH

TISHBE

ZAPHON

```
M T N B C O B B A A L G A D D
H A D A M B J E K E N A T H I
A B C P O E B A Z M M M I S B
H B U H K N T A Z E U A S B O
E A I Q A A H A B E R W H O N
B T L L R E B U T B R D B H K
G H H O A E R N O M A K E E N
O I T Z D S H U Q N J R T R M
J H H E A E A Z S Y O B O H I
C I M A G B B R A G N E N T A
B R E O R A O A E P Y O I E N
E D R E I M N L R G H N M B A
Q P E L L A I S R E R O V M H
W K H A R M I N H T E B N F A
C K I R I A T H A I M O K L M
```

◇ Bonus Trivia

Twenty was the minimum age for serving in
the Israelite army. Number 1:3

387

Word Search 193

NEW TESTAMENT PRACTICES

ASSEMBLY	MERCY
BAPTISM	OBEY
BOLDNESS	PEACE
COMFORT	PERSEVERE
COMMUNION	PRAYER
CONSOLE	PURITY
ENDURE	SALVATION
FAITH	SERVICE
FAST	STEADFAST
FELLOWSHIP	STUDY
FOOTWASHING	TESTIFY
GIVE	THANKS
HOPE	TITHE
HUMBLE	TRUTH
JUST	WITNESS
LOVE	WORK

```
C O M M U N I O N I P T J E F
S A L V A T I O N E R U R F B
S S E N D L O B R O S U H A G
F R Y E B O E S F T D P P S N
A Y D U T S E M R N I T T T I
I W O R K V O E E H I B I S H
T A P I E C Y Z S S C T T E S
H J E R T A D W M O E S H R A
G L E R R S O Y N S H A E V W
K I U P K L C S T S P F H I T
U T V N L R O I P E U D U C O
H L A E E L F E P N R A M E O
W H F M E Y A O B T I E B B F
T L O V E C H E E I T T L X P
A A S S E M B L Y W Y S E L H
```

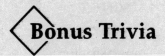

Bonus Trivia

Abraham was 100 when Isaac was born.
Genesis 21:5

Word Search 194

NAMES, TITLES, & OFFICES OF GOD

ADON	LORD
ADONAI	MKADDESH
ALMIGHTY	NISSI
ANCIENT OF DAYS	OLAM
DELIVERER	PRINCE
EL	RAPHA
ELAH	REFUGE
ELOHIM	ROHI
ELYON	SABOATH
FATHER	SAVIOR
GIBBOR	SHADDAI
IMMANUEL	SHALOM
JEHOVAH	SHELTER
JESUS	SON
JIREH	TSIDKENU
KING	WONDERFUL

```
D L D E L Y O N O K B A R I O
S O M F A T H E R I J N O S A
O R A Y T H G I M L A C H S Y
N D A H P A R M O L L I I I Z
M U S A B O A T H U U E R N Z
K M N B S N U Y F H O N E O H
A O T E U K S R A A M T F L I
D L E E K A E V S D I O U A A
D A L C V D O A H O H F G M D
E H D I N H I N E N O D E E D
S S O O E I Z S L A L A L T A
H R W J N U R L T I E Y A D H
B L E L A H E P E E Z S V J S
B H G I B B O R R Y J E S U S
R E R E V I L E D U D G N I K
```

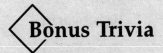

Bonus Trivia

Pharaoh gave Joseph an Egyptian name —
Zaphenath-Paneah. Genesis 41:45

Word Search 195

GOD IS . . .

BLESSED	LIFE
CLEAN	LIGHT
ENDURING	LOVE
ETERNAL	MERCIFUL
EVERLASTING	ONE
FAITHFUL	PATIENT
GLORIFIED	PEACE
GRACIOUS	PRINCE
GREAT	REFUGE
HOLY	RIGHTEOUS
HUMBLE	TRUE
IMMORTAL	TRUTH
IMMUTABLE	UPRIGHT
JUST	WISE
KIND	WONDERFUL
KING	

```
L A T R O M M I O D T Y F E R
U N G T T R U E N N D E L B I
F G R S X F H R E E A B T L G
H N E U R P E I I M A R E E H
T I A J R F T F E T U C V S T
I K T I U A I R U T A A F S E
A D N G P R C M H E C J K E O
F C E Y O I M G P E Z L T D U
E J L L F I Q M N H L U E W S
E O G U D E S I W I G B V A E
H F L N S U O I C A R G M V N
G N I T S A L R E V E U O U O
H K H L E T E R N A L L D M H
W S P W O N D E R F U L Y N P
I U P R I G H T L I G H T A E
```

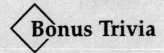

Bonus Trivia

After the frogs that plagued Egypt died, they
were put in big piles and made a real stink.
Exodus 8:32

Word Search 196

FIRST PEOPLE, PLACES, & THINGS

ABEL	JESUS
ABRAHAM	LAMECH
ADAM	LEAH
ANTIOCH	MACHPELAH
BARNABAS	MELCHIZEDEK
CAIN	NAAMAH
CANA	NIGHT
DAY	NOAH
EDEN	OTHNIEL
ELEAZER	PAUL
ENOCH	PETER
ESAU	RACHEL
ESTHER	RAVEN
EUTYCHUS	REBEKAH
EVE	RUTH
GOD	SAUL
GREEN	SERPENT
JACOB	SOLOMON
JAMES	

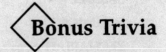

Bonus Trivia

Kings went to war in the spring.
2 Samuel 11:1

Word Search 197

BIBLE BY-LINES

AGUR	JUDE
AMOS	LEMUEL
ASAPH	LUKE
DANIEL	MALACHI
DAVID	MARK
ETHAN	MATTHEW
EZEKIEL	MICAH
EZRA	MOSES
HABAKKUK	NAHUM
HAGGAI	NEHEMIAH
HEMAN	OBADIAH
HOSEA	PAUL
ISAIAH	PETER
JAMES	SAMUEL
JEREMIAH	SOLOMON
JOEL	ZECHARIAH
JOHN	ZEPHANIAH
JOSHUA	

```
M I C A H J H E M A N S V G H
I S A I A H A T M B J N C M A
Z K F M F N J U S A D U A V I
E B E S A E L L H K R T D P R
P S O H T E E W U S T K S E A
H M U H U M I K L H O S E A H
A M A M U D K G E I N J L E C
N N A E I A E W I Q A L A Z E
I S L V B N Z S N N T G M R Z
A P A A A O E E A V U A G A Y
H D H P A M L S D R L L U A P
C L N E S O I O B A D I A H H
F E H T A L C M C L U K E N D
G O O E P O X H A I M E R E J
A J J R H S I N E H E M I A H
```

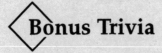

Bonus Trivia

Paul was from the tribe of Benjamin.
Romans 11:1

Word Search 198

INSECTS, SNAKES, RODENTS, ETC.

ANT	LOCUST
ASP	MICE
BEE	MOLE
BEETLE	MOTH
CANKERWORM	MOUSE
CRICKET	NEHUSHTAN
FLEA	RAT
FLY	SCORPION
GNAT	SERPENT
GOPHER	SKINK
GRASSHOPPER	SLUG
HORNET	SNAI
KATYDID	SPIDER
LEECH	VIPER
LEVIATHAN	WORM
LICE	

```
T S U C O L K T Q K W S L U G
W B R J W W A E L F A D R V E
E Z E H A O T S Y L I E S C L
S S D O Y R Y A E A P N E A T
K F I R L M D V N P R N R N E
I L P N F X I S O U C A P K E
N I S E P A D H K T K T E E B
K C H T T H S S R H G H N R G
X E N H G S C C C T O S T W N
I A A T A O R E Z O P U P O A
U N A R R I X E E M H H S R T
N R G P C P K S S L E E E M O
U V I K S M U S D Q R N E H N
G O E A V O V I P E R C B B L
N T O N M E C I M H M O L E N
```

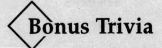

Bonus Trivia

The priest who offered a burnt offering for
someone got to keep the hide. Leviticus 7:8

Word Search 199

WATER: IN IT & ON IT

ALTAR

ANANIAS

APOLLOS

ARK

AXHEAD

BARNABUS

BARSABUS

BARTHOLOMEW

CORNELIUS

DISCIPLES

EPHESIANS

EUNUCH

FLEECE

JAMES

JOHN

JOSEPH

LUKE

MARK

MARY

MATTHEW

MATTHIAS

NICHOLAS

NOAH

PAUL

PETER

PHILIP

SILAS

SIMON

STEPHEN

THADDEUS

THOMAS

TIMON

WORLD

ZELOTES

```
H M M P C I V B A R N A B U S
Z E C E H J O S E P H L M E V
T D I S C I P L E S W L A P N
I C O R N E L I U S E X R H V
M H L U A P E I X I M T Y E Z
O D A E H X A L P M O H B S E
N N T H O M A S F O L A A I L
V N I C H O L A S N O D R A O
G S H C U N U E I J H D S N T
A T W E H T T A M A T E A S E
R E S A I H T T A M R U B R S
K P M I L N H O J E A S U A L
U H S O L L O P A S B O S T U
R E T E P A B A D L R O W L K
A N A N I A S G H M A R K A E
```

Bonus Trivia

Nothing in Solomon's house was made of silver because it wasn't worth much then.
1 Kings 10:21

Word Search 200

GOD ASKED WHO?

ABRAHAM	JEWS
ADAM	JOB
AHAB	JOHN
BARTIMAEUS	JONAH
CAIN	JOSHUA
CYRUS	LAWYER
DAVID	MANOAH
DISCIPLES	MARTHA
EVE	MOSES
EZEKIEL	PAUL
HERODIANS	PETER
ISAIAH	PHARISEES
JACOB	PHILIP
JAMES	SADUCEES
JEREMIAH	SAMUEL

```
P H I L I P P H A R I S E E S
S S P S E L P I C S I D S D S
L E U M A S J S S I D J E I E
Y Q W P X O H U U Z U S M V S
J N R G S E E R E P G A A A O
O H H H R R R Y A T D L J D M
N E U O E B O C M A H U L S Y
A A M Y J O D V I M A A H A M
H P W X A C I E T A I P A D A
I A M H U A A O R H M A I U R
L B A L E J N Y A A E C A C T
Z B N O Y G S B B R R A S E H
M J O B K S W E J B E I I E A
F X A R E T E P Z A J N Q S Q
P V H N N E V E Z E K I E L P
```

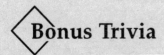

Bonus Trivia

Solomon wrote 3,000 proverbs and 1,005
songs. 1 Kings 4:32

Answers

Puzzle #1

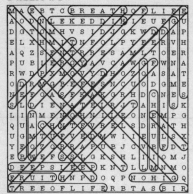

Puzzle #2

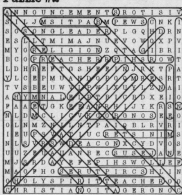

Puzzle #3

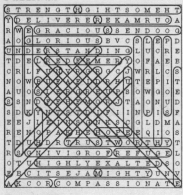

Puzzle #4

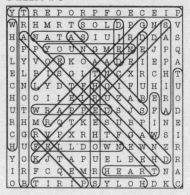

Puzzle #5

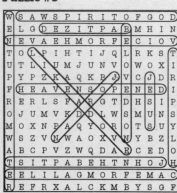

Puzzle #6

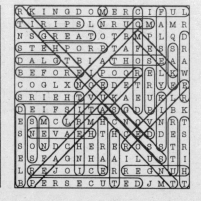

Puzzle #7

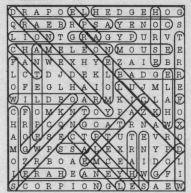

Puzzle #8

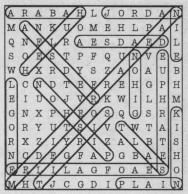

Puzzle #9

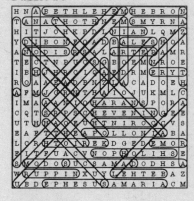

Puzzle #10

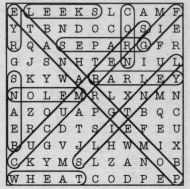

Puzzle #11

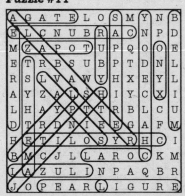

Puzzle #12

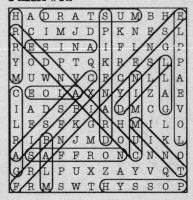

Puzzle #13

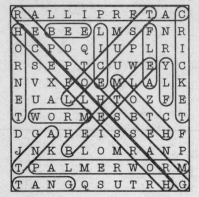

Puzzle #14

Puzzle #15

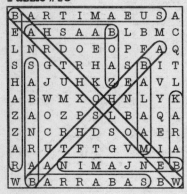

Puzzle #16

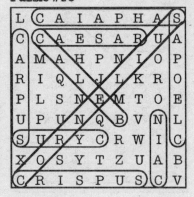

Puzzle #17

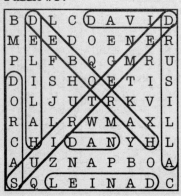

Puzzle #18

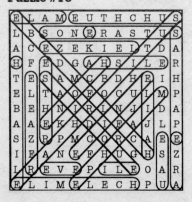

Puzzle #19

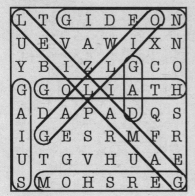

```
L T G I D E O N
U E V A W I X N
Y B I Z L G C O
G G O L I A T H
A D A P A D Q S
I G E S R M F R
U T G V H U A E
S M O H S R E G
```

Puzzle #20

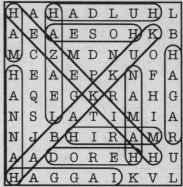

```
H A H A D L U H L
A E A E S O H K B
M C Z M D N U O H
H E A E P K N F A
A Q E G K R A H G
N S L A T I M I A
N J B H I R A M R
A A D O R E H H U
H A G G A I K V L
```

Puzzle #21

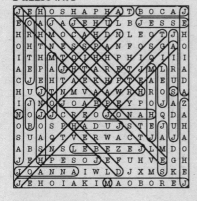

```
J E H O S H A P H A T B O C A J
E O A J A J E H U L B J E S S E
H R H M O C A H D N L E O T J H
O H T N E S S P A N F O S G A I
I T H M T O I H P H I Q L I R J
A P A J T A R E T J M A L E O T
C H J E H T A E K H P T E A E O A
H U J T N M V A A W R H O R O J
I J N O J O A E P E Y P O J A Z
N O B J J C R E O J X O N A H Q D
O B O S P H A D U J S T E J A U
S U A C T V E R W A C T J A J A
A B S N S L E B E Z E J L M D O
J E H P E S O J E F U H V E G H
J O A N N A I W L D J X M S K E
J E H O I A K I M A O B O R E J
```

Puzzle #22

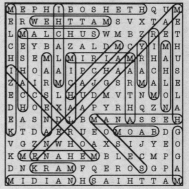

```
M E P H I B O S H E T H Q U M
E R W E H T T A M S V X T A E
L M A L C H U S W M B Z R E T
C E Y B A Z A L D M C Y I M H
H S E M L M I E I A M R H U U
I H O A A I P C H A A A C L S
Z A I R M C A J G S R M A L E
D H O E X A A P Y R H Q Z N L
E A S N D L B M A N A S S E H
K T D A E R U E O M O A B D G
V G Z N W H O A X S I J Y E O
K M E N A H E M B L E C M P G A
D N K R A M F Q E R O S G P A
M I D I A N H S A I H T T A M
```

Puzzle #23

```
N A P H T A L I A N A H O R
B E H K N P C N I L O D A
N A H A S H E A J M E Z G N
Q Y F E R Z G D S A Z T B A
U C H J M V D A W E I E X C
S K R W Z I L B N M S N T I
U N U X A O A D P V Y A Q N
M N A O M I A H B H K H C A
E D I L C H E J O E N U G H
D M R T C N T H O A P M S T
O U A U V B C O M W N C X A
C Y B D G E Z A B E H O F N
J E I R N J A O S A K P A L
N A T H A N A E L M N Q N H
```

Puzzle #24

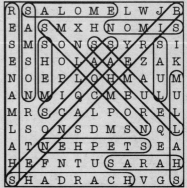

```
R S A L O M E L W J B
E A S M X H N O M I S
A M S O N S S Y R S I
E S H O L A A E Z A K
N O N E P L O H M A U M
A N M I Q C M B U L U
M R S C A L P O R E L
L S O N S D M S N Q L
A T N E H P E T S E A
H E F N T U S A R A H
S H A D R A C H V G S
```

Puzzle #25

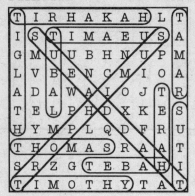

Puzzle #26

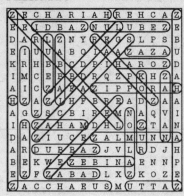

Puzzle #27

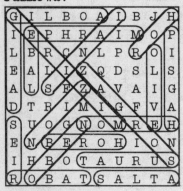

Puzzle #28

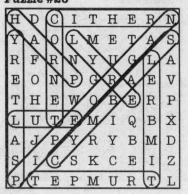

Puzzle #29

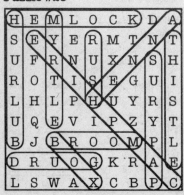

Puzzle #30

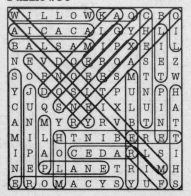

Puzzle #31

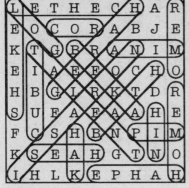

Puzzle #32

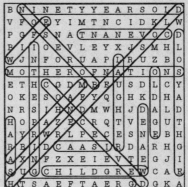

Puzzle #33

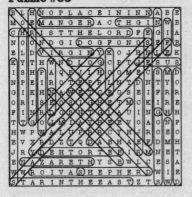

Puzzle #34

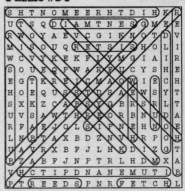

Puzzle #35

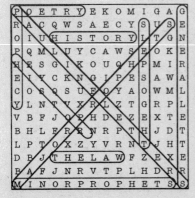

Puzzle #36

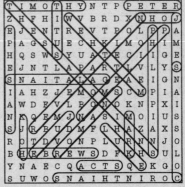

Puzzle #37

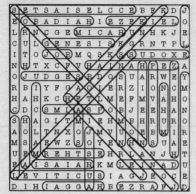

Puzzle #38

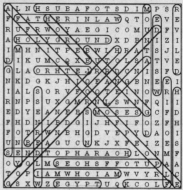

Puzzle #39

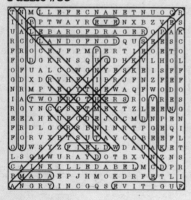

Puzzle #40

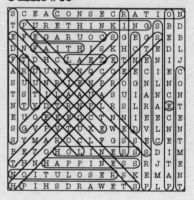

Puzzle #41

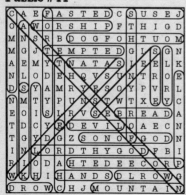

Puzzle #42

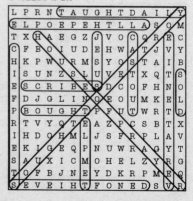

Puzzle #43

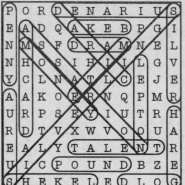

Puzzle #44

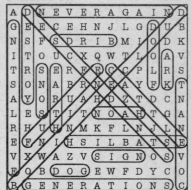

Puzzle #45

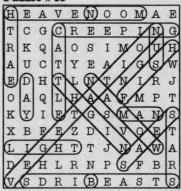

Puzzle #46

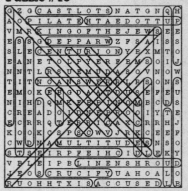

Puzzle #47

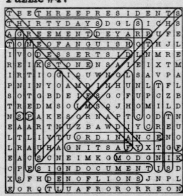

Puzzle #48

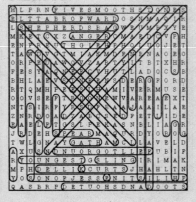

Puzzle #49

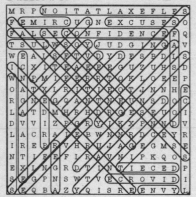

Puzzle #50

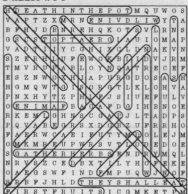

Puzzle #51

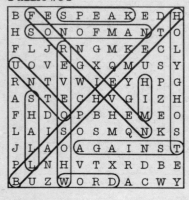

Puzzle #52

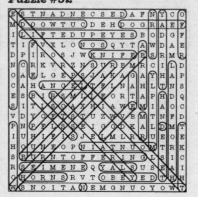

Puzzle #53

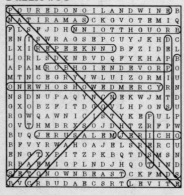

Puzzle #54

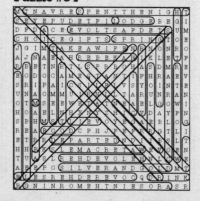

Puzzle #55

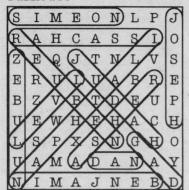

Puzzle #56

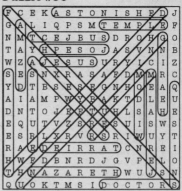

Puzzle #57

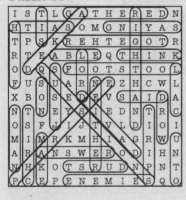

Puzzle #58

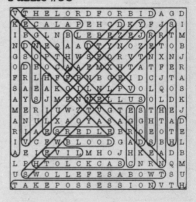

Puzzle #59

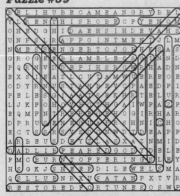

Puzzle #60

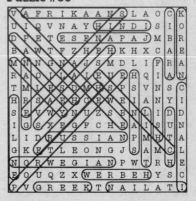

Puzzle #61

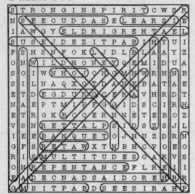

Puzzle #62

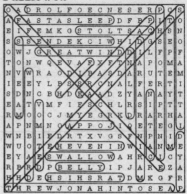

Puzzle #63

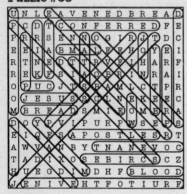

Puzzle #64

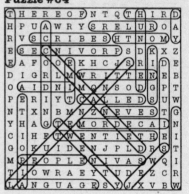

Puzzle #65

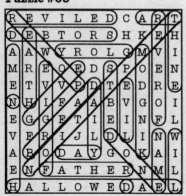

Puzzle #66

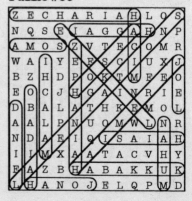

Puzzle #67

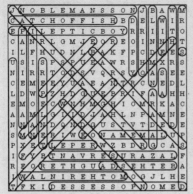

Puzzle #68

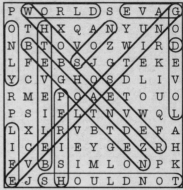

Puzzle #69

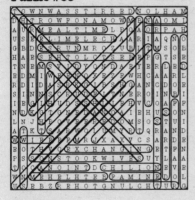

Puzzle #70

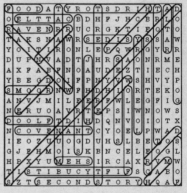

Puzzle #71

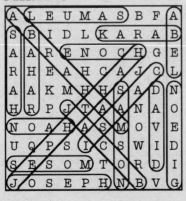

Puzzle #72

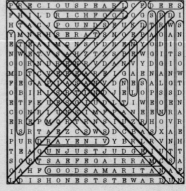

Puzzle #73

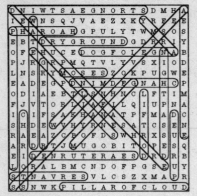

Puzzle #74

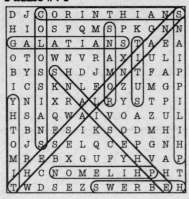

Puzzle #75

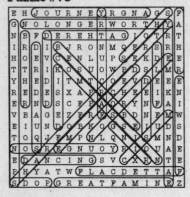

Puzzle #76

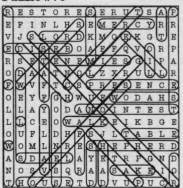

Puzzle #77

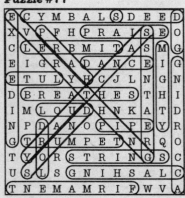

Puzzle #78

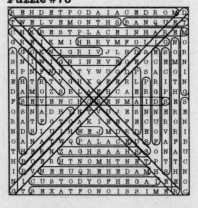

Puzzle #79

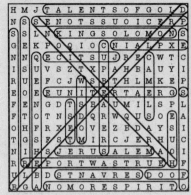

Puzzle #80

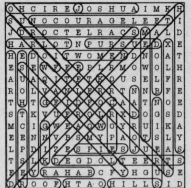

Puzzle #81

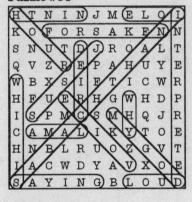

Puzzle #82

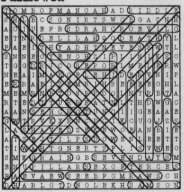

Puzzle #83

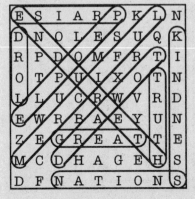

Puzzle #84

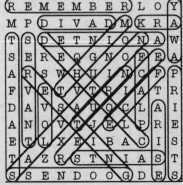

Puzzle #85

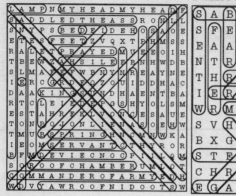

Puzzle #86

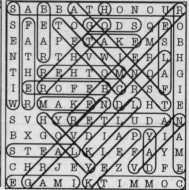

Puzzle #87

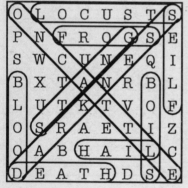

Puzzle #88

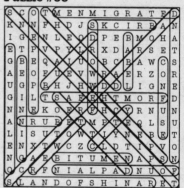

Puzzle #89

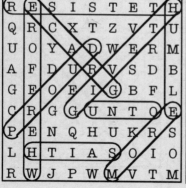

Puzzle #90

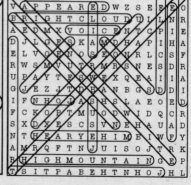

Puzzle #91

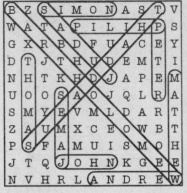

Puzzle #92

Puzzle #93

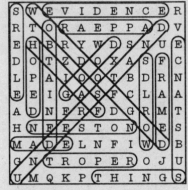

Puzzle #94

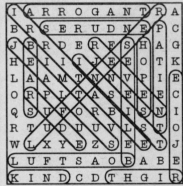

Puzzle #95

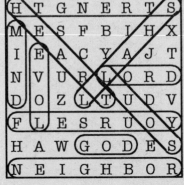

Puzzle #96

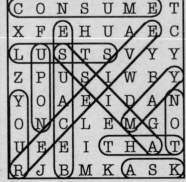

419

Puzzle #97

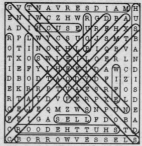

Puzzle #98

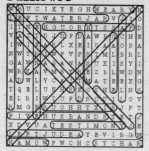

Puzzle #99

Puzzle #100

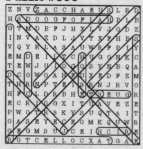

Puzzle #101

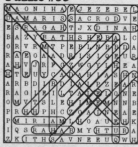

Puzzle #102

Puzzle #103

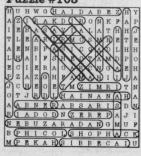

Puzzle #104

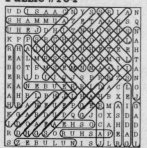

Puzzle #105

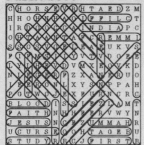

Puzzle #106

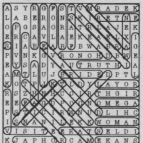

Puzzle #107

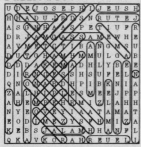

Puzzle #108

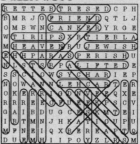

Puzzle #109

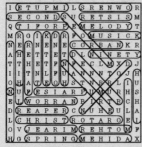

Puzzle #110

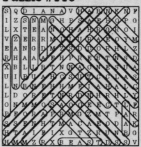

Puzzle #111

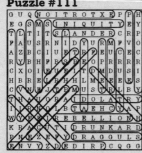

Puzzle #112

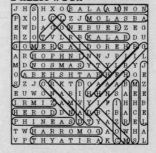

Puzzle #113

Puzzle #114

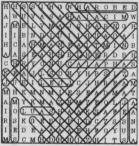

Puzzle #115

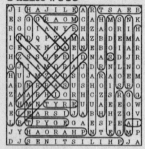

Puzzle #116

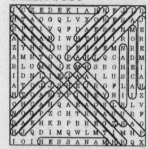

Puzzle #117

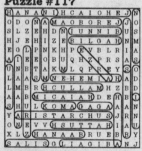

Puzzle #118

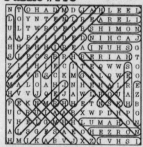

Puzzle #119

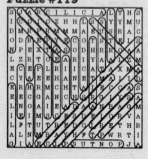

Puzzle #120

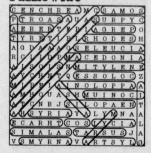

422

Puzzle #121

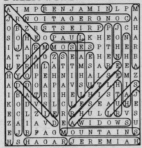

Puzzle #122

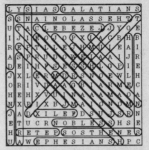

Puzzle #123

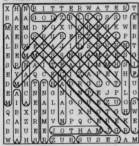

Puzzle #124

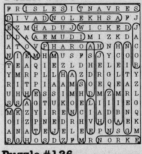

Puzzle #125

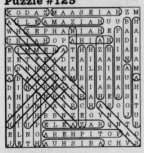

Puzzle #126

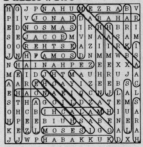

Puzzle #127

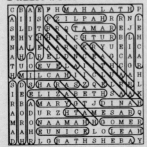

Puzzle #128

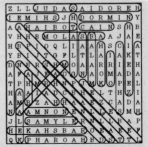

423

Puzzle #129

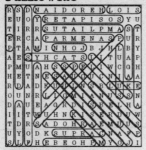

Puzzle #130

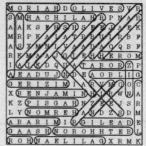

Puzzle #131

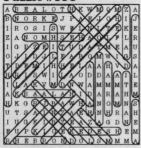

Puzzle #132

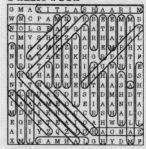

Puzzle #133

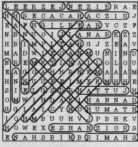

Puzzle #134

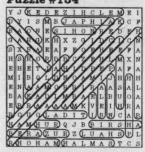

Puzzle #135

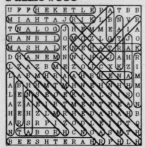

Puzzle #136

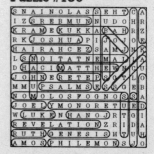

Puzzle #137

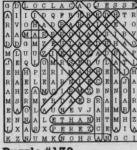

Puzzle #138

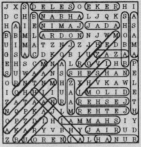

Puzzle #139

Puzzle #140

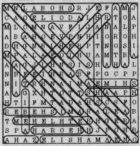

Puzzle #141

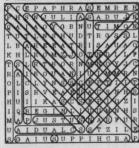

Puzzle #142

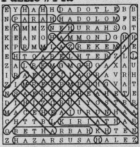

Puzzle #143

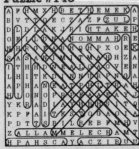

Puzzle #144

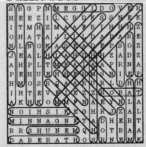

Puzzle #145

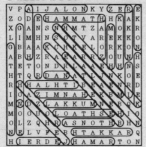

Puzzle #146

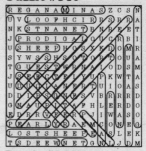

Puzzle #147

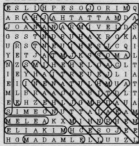

Puzzle #148

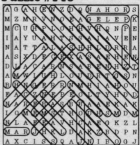

Puzzle #149

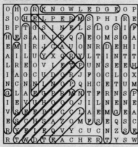

Puzzle #150

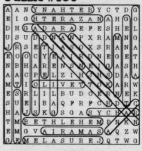

Puzzle #151

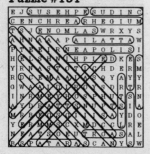

Puzzle #152

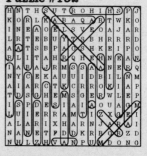

426

Puzzle #153

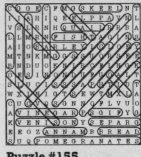

Puzzle #154

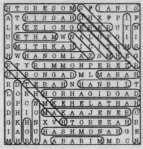

Puzzle #155

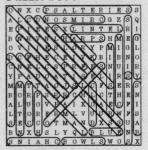

Puzzle #156

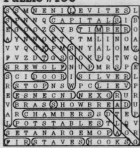

Puzzle #157

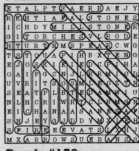

Puzzle #158

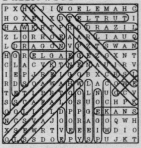

Puzzle #159

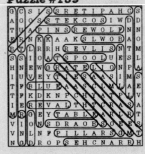

Puzzle #160

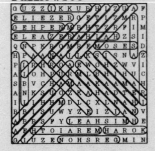

Puzzle #161

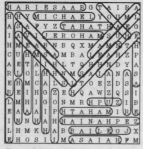

Puzzle #162

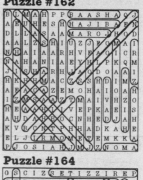

Puzzle #163

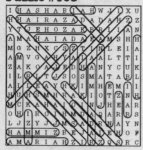

Puzzle #164

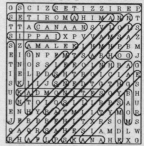

Puzzle #165

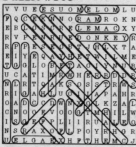

Puzzle #166

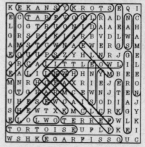

Puzzle #167

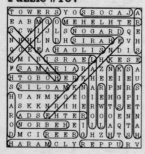

Puzzle #168

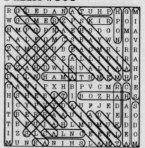

Puzzle #169

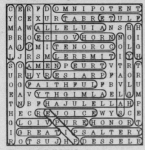

Puzzle #170

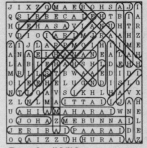

Puzzle #171

Puzzle #172

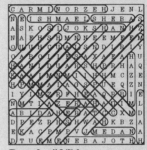

Puzzle #173

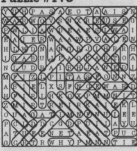

Puzzle #174

Puzzle #175

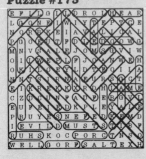

Puzzle #176

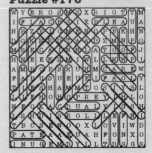

Puzzle #177

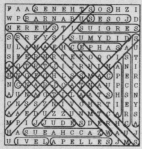

Puzzle #178

Puzzle #179

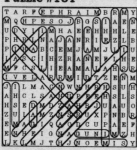

Puzzle #180

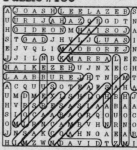

Puzzle #181

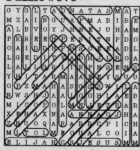

Puzzle #182

Puzzle #183

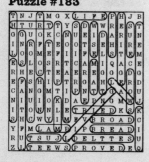

Puzzle #184

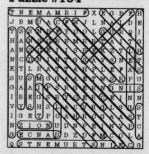

430

Puzzle #185

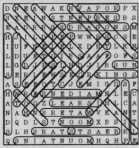

Puzzle #186

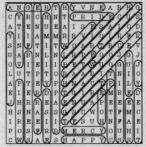

Puzzle #187

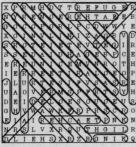

Puzzle #188

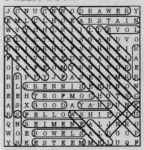

Puzzle #189

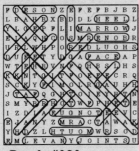

Puzzle #190

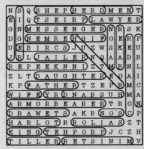

Puzzle #191

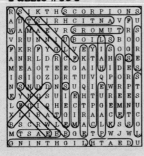

Puzzle #192

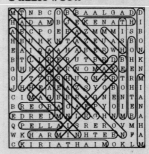

Puzzle #193

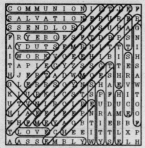

Puzzle #194

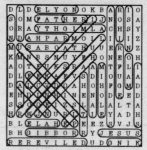

Puzzle #195

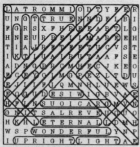

Puzzle #196

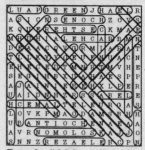

Puzzle #197

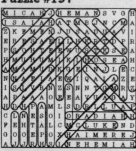

Puzzle #198

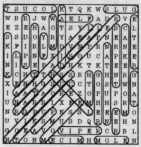

Puzzle #199

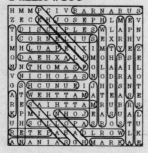

Puzzle #200

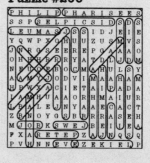